Even in Summer the
Ice Doesn't Melt

Even in Summer the

Ice Doesn't Melt

DAVID K. REYNOLDS, PH.D.

QUILL
WILLIAM MORROW
NEW YORK

Library of Congress Cataloging-in-Publication Data

Reynolds, David K.
    Even in summer the ice doesn't melt.

    Bibliography: p.
    1. Morita psychotherapy.   2. Naikan psychotherapy.
3. Neuroses—Treatment.   I. Title.
RC489.M65R47   1986   616.89'14   86-12260
ISBN 0-688-06744-1

Printed in the United States of America

To my students—my teachers

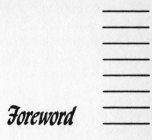

Foreword

A suggestion for all Western readers, but particularly for professionals in the fields of psychology, psychotherapy, and counseling: Try to read this book (and others based on Morita therapy and Naikan) line by line, resisting the tendency to fill in the contents with familiar concepts. These systems are quite radically different from any others in the West. On the surface there may be superficial similarities reminding us of our pet Western theories and methods. But I assure you that the underlying way of looking at neurosis and cure presented here is fundamentally divergent from anything we have in the West. Unless carefully watched, your mind will make translations of what you read that will make the contents readily understandable but no longer what Morita or Yoshimoto intended, or what I wrote.

When you read below that we all have multiple personalities, that therapy shouldn't aim at the reduction of anxiety and depression, that every unpleasant "symptom" comes from a positive desire, that feelings are directly uncontrollable, that no one knows why we behave as we do, that change can only come about "now," that what we attend to is all that we know in any given moment, and that grief totally disappears when we don't pay attention to it, remember that the words were chosen carefully. Please consider these ideas not in terms of the way the mind ought to be or the way you have been taught that the mind operates, but rather in terms of how your own mind actually functions. Examine these Eastern notions in terms of your own experiential recognition—a level below that of psychological theory. For Western psychological theory grew, or should have grown, from this very level of recognition in some psychological theorist's life.

We are considering here a revolutionary idea, new to Western psychotherapy and personal development. Anxiety, depression, fear, grief, worries, self-doubts, and the like are no longer to be considered solely in terms of their unpleasantness, but rather the emphasis will be on their naturalness. They aren't to be disposed of; they are to be accepted, used, and put on a shelf while we get on about doing what needs doing in life.

A case can be made that this way of handling life's suffering is nothing other than a secularized form of Buddhism, a psychologized version of Buddhist thought. Some scholars would be content to so categorize this lifeway and then to dismiss it without any consideration of its personal implications for them or its wider implications for therapy and healthful living in the West. My hope is that you will see the shortsightedness of such vision by the time you have finished reading this book.

In Zen it is said that the firewood never becomes ashes. There is truth in that saying. Now firewood, now ashes.

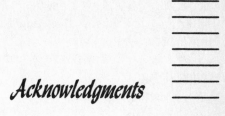

Acknowledgments

Mr. Yozo Hasegawa, director of the Moritist organization called Seikatsu no Hakkenkai, has taught me much about the theory and history of Morita therapy in Japan, about constructive living, and about teaching this lifeway through word and example.

Dr. Hiromu Shimbo and his family continue to provide accommodations, wise counsel, and supporting friendship during my annual periods of study in Japan. Mrs. Mali Kikuchi faithfully translates my writings into Japanese text that is consistently superior to my original work, allowing wide feedback from Japanese colleagues.

Practical encouragement and thoughtful suggestions based on Naikan thought in Japan are contributed each year by Mr. Ishin Yoshimoto and the Reverend Shue Usami and their wives, and by Professor Akira Ishii of Aoyama Gakuin University.

The families of Mr. Shigetada Tamashiro and Dr. Brian Ogawa provide accommodations and examples of constructive living during my annual work periods in Hawaii. I am indeed fortunate to be surrounded and supported in Los Angeles, Hawaii, and Japan by living examples of this approach to living.

Not all Japanese live according to the principles of Morita therapy or Naikan. In fact, very few do. Special people are special people in any culture. But the presence of these lifeways fosters the possibility of constructive lives of service. The potential impact of even this possibility shouldn't be underestimated.

Finally, to Lynn, who gives me the freedom to travel with mind and luggage, and to my students, teachers, and friends of the Pacific Basin, who make the traveling worthwhile, a formal expression of gratitude. Always they taught well; sometimes I failed to learn their lessons.

I am merely Reality's way of getting certain work done that needed doing.

Contents

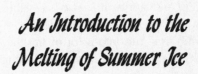

An Introduction to the Melting of Summer Ice

In this world there are a very few people who *know* what they are talking about and a great many people who talk about *them*. Two people who belong in the category of those-who-know are Shoma Morita and Ishin Yoshimoto. This book is a blending of their thoughts and approaches to warming humans who suffer from icy despair, chilling anxiety, blizzards of self-doubt, and the slush of self-centeredness.

I have written several books introducing these Eastern growth methods to Western readers. Those of you who are already familiar with the basic principles of Morita's method and Yoshimoto's Naikan may wish to skip this introductory chapter and move on to the new material that follows it.

What I have called elsewhere "constructive living" and "playing ball on running water" (see References) is a way of approaching life with attention to what is controllable and what is not. The sensible person doesn't waste time and energy trying to control feelings directly, for example, because they can't be manipulated directly by the will. We can't make ourselves feel confident or satisfied or grateful or loving or courageous just by concentrating or wishing we were so. Try it. It doesn't work with any consistency at all.

On the other hand, provided we don't have some physical

handicap, most of us can will our bodies to wash dishes and the body obeys. We can force ourselves to go for job interviews, make speeches, exercise, get up in the morning, and so forth *even when we don't feel like it.* Of course, it's a lot easier to do what we feel like doing, but life doesn't always bring us a neat package of pleasant feelings and matching behavior. Part of maturity is taking responsibility for what we do, no matter what we are feeling. It turns out that this attitude toward responsibility in behavior is not only an element of maturity, it is also a sensible approach to living with real payoff in everyday life. People who try to "go with their feelings" all the time run into a lot of trouble.

So do people who try to control their feelings. Some people try to extend the notion of responsibility for what they do (behavior) into the realm of emotions or feelings. That approach is a mistake. We can't control what we feel. We aren't bad for feeling anything—sexy feelings, lazy feelings, angry feelings, depressed feelings, confused feelings, any feelings. The best strategy for handling a feeling, any feeling, is to accept it as it is (without trying to fight it directly in any way) and go on about doing what life presents us to do. The feeling, in time, will pass and be replaced by some other feeling. No feeling lasts in its intensity forever.

It is true, however, that we can sometimes indirectly influence how we feel by being careful about what we do. Reading pornography (behavior) stimulates sex-related emotions (feelings); avoiding elevators (behavior) stimulates increased fear of elevators (feelings); failing to wash and dress in the morning (behavior) encourages low self-esteem and laziness (feelings); jogging (behavior) produces energy and then tiredness (feelings); and so forth. A warning: These behaviors, like any other behaviors, don't always result in the feelings we want or expect. There is *no* way to control feelings with any certainty and consistency. So the monitoring of life, the steadiness of life, the sense of control in life, must come from our behavior, from what we do. Check out your own experience. Isn't it so? You haven't been able to hold on to good feelings. You haven't had great success making unpleasant

DAVID K. REYNOLDS

feelings go away when you wished. But sometimes, in spite of moments of misery and euphoria and all sorts of feelings in between, you accomplished what you set out to do in those moments. Sometimes your behavior held steady in spite of turbulence in your emotional life. It was in those times that your feelings settled down relatively quickly. The more you give yourself up to wild extremes of behavior in order to match your extreme feelings, the more you perpetuate the strong emotions. Look back and think about some recent event in your life from this point of view. Can you see it?

It is easy for us to fool ourselves into believing that we are in control of our personal worlds. But there are reminders that we are not when we push a button or turn a key or flip a switch and what we expected to happen does not. Go into the wilderness for a while and learn again how little we control of the world. Look at storms, at dying, at the land unplowed and unpaved. After viewing our impotence it becomes more reasonable to ask the situation what needs to be done rather than trying to impose our will on it. It makes more sense to accept our feelings as they are, just as we had to accept the snow and the lightning and the waterfall and the sunset.

We aren't taught these simple principles of living in our formal education: Feelings are not directly controllable by our wills; feelings fade over time unless we do something to restimulate them; we needn't let our feelings dominate our behavior; behavior sometimes indirectly influences feelings; we can accomplish many of our purposes in life in spite of our feelings; feelings can be accepted as they are; we have no responsibility for what we feel; we are responsible for what we do no matter what we are feeling; and there are others. You can read a more detailed treatment of this subject in *Constructive Living* and *Playing Ball on Running Water*. Those books also offer exercises for putting the principles into practice in everyday life, as well as maxims and fairy tale allegories to help keep the principles in mind.

Part of our unnecessary distress comes from a sort of self-centeredness or self-focus that turns our attention inward to notice all our negative feelings. We freeze our actions and our self-image in this way. When we can lose ourselves in our surroundings (in our work, in our companions, in our observations of the ever-shifting world that presents itself to us) we become fluid again, fitting ourselves appropriately to the situation at hand. One of the ways we learn to thaw ourselves from our icy neurotic bonds is to discover (or rediscover) how we are "lived" by the world about us.

What is really mine? Not my body—it was given to me by my parents and by their parents, nourished by the food they fed me, food grown by others and processed by others whose names I don't even know. Not my mind—the ideas were loaned to me by teachers and authors and parents and students and friends; and the ideas well up out of nowhere and are replaced by other ideas drifting through my mind unbidden. Not my words—taught to me by others, created and revised from ancient times; again, appearing from nowhere, imprinting on the screen of my mind. Not my books or my car or my home or my clothes; not my name or my friends or my colleagues or my culture or my time—all loaned to me . . . and to you. Trace out the debts in detail. The myth of the self-made person is bankrupt.

One of the exercises we suggest to our clients is to reflect upon and write in detail on a daily basis what they have received from significant others in their lives (parents, spouses, children, teachers, friends, and the like), what they have returned to those people, and what troubles they have caused those loved ones. Note that the troubles caused by the loved ones is not one of the themes for reflection. Why is it that we tend to dwell upon the troubles others have caused us, and to fail to notice and to forget quickly the inconvenience and trouble we cause them? Again, the details of such an assignment are written elsewhere; the point here is that another way to thaw ourselves is to recognize the warmth that creates us, surrounds us, and quite literally sustains us moment by moment.

The result of such recognition is a feeling of gratitude and a desire to repay our debt to the world through service to those around us. Somewhere within that process we forget ourselves and the icicles of misery melt. It isn't that we are never troubled again. It is just that for the moments we give up ourselves we have transcended our troubles. Looked at up close a thumbnail is enormous. At arm's length it takes on a different perspective.

People ask the way to Hanshan,
But there is no way to Hanshan.
The ice does not melt even in summer,
And even if the sun should rise,
Dense vapours clothe it 'round.
—KANZAN

ESSASYS

Sometimes This, Sometimes That

I dislike being told how I must be feeling. Locked out of my office one day I remember feeling inconvenienced but not particularly angry. A colleague insisted that I must have been angry—after all, someone had forgotten to tell me about the change of locks. But I wasn't angry, I insisted. Sometimes I'm angry, to be sure, but not that time. He persisted: I must have been very angry to deny and repress it so strongly. I wonder.

Sometimes we feel pressured by psychological theory or by friends or therapists or spouses to own up to emotions that they insist must be there. When someone pulls out from the curb in front of my car without any signal and I am forced to brake suddenly, then sometimes I am upset and sometimes not. There seems to be no purpose in digging for anger that someone else believes must be hidden somewhere in my psyche. If I am denying and repressing the feeling, why do I recognize and affirm it sometimes? Why should I try to fit my experience to someone else's theoretical satisfaction?

It is the same with speaking before large audiences. Sometimes I am more tense than at other times. Sometimes I feel more courageous and less shy than at other times. Aren't you the same? When we reflect back on our childhood, weren't we sometimes angry at our parents and sometimes appreciative of them, sometimes satisfied with our lot and sometimes intensely dissatisfied, sometimes loving and sometimes hating? To talk about an unhappy childhood is to oversimplify the complexity of the past in order to fit some current need. We may want to consider ourselves deprived as children so that we can explain our current limitations. We may want to emphasize our feelings of abandonment as children in order to please some sort of counselor who, we hope, can ultimately make some organized sense of our lives. I wonder.

The simplified explanations of life built upon uncaring fathers and overprotective mothers and expectable feelings may have some value because they make us believe that we have a handle on why we are the way we are. But they aren't true. I'm really very sorry to put it so bluntly. They aren't true. They are simple fairy tales about who we were and are. The reality is so much richer and more complex than these caricatures that a little genuine reflection will show them to be imaginative scaffolds for reconstructing a safely understandable past. There may very well have been an overprotective mother in your past. But her existence is no single-variable explanation of your lack of self-confidence or your current difficulties with your office pals or your fights with the kids. What you felt then and what you feel now and what you will feel tomorrow are so complexly determined (as much by what you have done as by what others have done to you) that to buy into any simple psychodynamic explanatory system is rather childlike and naïve.

It occurs to me that the news media have helped perpetuate these oversimplified views of ourselves and our world. When I am interviewed on television the newsperson or talk show host wants to know *the* problem with mental hospitals. What is *the* cause of neurotic suffering? What are *the* three reasons why people kill themselves? Broadcast time and print space are limited. The complexities of reality aren't what people want to hear and read—or so many media people seem to think. Television, radio, and newspapers seem always to need something immediate, something unusual. News shows meet that need, as do sports events and call-in shows with topical themes. Such programming is ephemeral. It

DAVID K. REYNOLDS

isn't expected to provide in-depth, lasting information. Instead, it will soon be replaced by spot reporting of other recent events. The long-term view, the history, the panorama, are relegated to a brief background statement. The result is an oversimplification in our understanding and in our approach to understanding. But there is a different area in which simplification is not only possible, but desirable.

Consider the possibility of simply accepting the feelings and moods and emotional reactions to events as they are. No need to try to make rational sense of them. No need to fathom their historical roots. No need to pause to reflect on whether they are normal or not. No need to examine what you ought to be feeling according to someone else's expectation. It is strange to call this perspective radical. But in this day and age it is radical to consider feelings to be natural phenomena, like temperature changes or leaves falling from trees in autumn. We would prefer that feelings be more like traffic lights—predictable, controllable, and dependable if we pace our lives properly and rationally. But the experience of emotion isn't mechanical in any simple way, like a traffic light. To try to exert direct control over our feelings based on some psychological understanding is, in any exact sense, fruitless.

So where does that perspective leave us? Are we destined to be buffeted about by every emotional gust? Can we make no sense at all of why we feel as we do? Are we doomed to passive resignation in the area of feelings? Not at all. Whatever perspective we adopt intellectually, we all continue to make some rough sense of why we are grouchy this morning, why we are tense when greeting the mailman today, why the tears came to our eyes during that movie episode. Our attempts to understand give us ideas about what we need to do in our lives, what needs to be changed in order to reduce or increase the likelihood of certain feelings. Nevertheless, there is a great deal of slippage between what we understand about our feelings and what actually causes the feelings. And there is slippage again between what we understand about our feelings and what we can and will do about the conditions that contribute to them. What I am arguing for here is, I suppose, a sort of humility about our feelings. With all our fine psychological theories we sometimes delude ourselves into believing that we really know a great deal about what is going on in our emotional lives. The emotional lives of not a few psychotherapists and counselors in my acquaintance belie this belief. We know very little. What is certain is that I am sometimes this, sometimes that. Sometimes pleased, sometimes not; sometimes confident, sometimes not; sometimes compassionate, sometimes not. The ice doesn't melt at my whim. It doesn't melt no matter how well I understand its origins or believe I understand its origins. It may not melt despite my persistent efforts to change the circumstances that I believe to be maintaining it. In such cases what else is there to do but shiver and go on about living?

Given that the above perspective more accurately describes what is going on in our affective or emotional lives, why go to the trouble to consider feelings from this unusual point of view? First, we no longer need to waste effort and energy trying for some elaborate intellectual insight. Some people will opt to seek psychodynamic insight whether it is practically useful or not, simply because it is interesting. No problem there. Positive and creative results can come to those who play with the symbols of the psyche. But that is not an endeavor of "cure," it is exploration. Second, the energy once devoted to seeking deep understanding of the hidden self can be redirected toward the more workable and controllable aspect of life—what we do. It isn't nearly as much fun to dig in and clean up our behavioral act, but the results are gratifying and dependable.

As a consequence of adopting this perspective on feelings we begin to accept them rather than trying to control, create, or dissolve them. We begin to see them as natural consequences of events sometimes recognized and sometimes not, but always natural. Natural means not good or bad. Just natural. When a lion kills and devours its prey it may not be a pretty sight, but the lion isn't bad for doing what it is natural for lions to do. Lions haven't the rational, thoughtful control over behavior that we humans can choose to assert over our own acts. A depression may be painful

DAVID K. REYNOLDS

to endure and hurtful to watch in someone else, but the hopeless and sorrow-filled feelings aren't bad. They are natural. We may use medication to ease the suffering (just as we may feed a caged lion), but there remains a degree of suffering that must be lived with while one gets on about shoveling away the snow on one's doorstep. And remarkably often, when we get involved in the shoveling, we lose sight of the sorrow and hopelessness.

This new point of view allows a freedom and self-acceptance of great depth. My feelings are an aspect of me. I don't need to understand them fully or to "solve" or to "dissolve" them somehow in order to get on with my life. I am the way I am, naturally. While working to improve my behavior there is no need to struggle with the doubts and obsessions and despair. They are all natural, just as they are. They aren't my responsibility; they are just passing through. I am not substandard or abnormal for having these thoughts and feelings. They are all right as they are. I am all right as I am. Now to get on with shoveling the walk.

The Third Factor

In my previous writings I have emphasized the relationship between feelings and behavior. Feelings are not directly controllable by the will and so must be accepted as they are; behavior is controllable, no matter what the feelings, and so involves responsibility, right and wrong. At this point I should like to introduce a third factor that influences and is influenced by feelings and behavior. The third factor is understanding.

The relationship among these three variables is quite complex. The purpose of this book, for example, is to guide your understanding. As you understand more about the limits and possibilities of your life your behavior will change. The changes in your behavior will, in turn, affect your understanding and your feelings. Changed feelings will influence your behavior, including what you read and talk about. What you read and talk about will have an impact on your understanding. Feelings will also influence what makes sense to you and what doesn't. So feelings will have a direct influence on your understanding. As your understanding becomes refined your attitudes toward yourself and others change; you become better able to see events from others' points of view. As a result, your feelings change.

Thus, there is a rich interaction among understanding, feelings, and behavior to effect changes in our lives. In this chapter I intend to focus on the ways in which proper understanding can change us in positive ways. We must distinguish here between intellectual knowledge and experiential understanding. The distinction is essentially the same as that between what the Japanese call *chishiki* or "knowledge" and what they call *chie* or "wisdom." Chishiki is structured, like a building. We construct it. In the case of knowledge we construct it with our intellects. Chishiki can be very organized, as in science. It can be helpful in controlling our world, providing machines and energy to serve us, for example. It can entertain us through novels and plays and films. Although it can be useful, it can also be wrong. It must be constantly updated, corrected. Like a building, chishiki needs constant repairs. It must change with the times.

Chie, on the other hand, is not constructed like a building. It is rather like an ocean. We don't create it, we immerse ourselves in it. Like lasting works of art or some elements of religious thought, chie is never outdated, never in need of repair. We discover chie not so much by thinking about it, not by pondering it, but by experiencing it. It remains true whether we recognize it or not. It keeps on existing, waiting for us to discover it.

For years I conducted recognized and sometimes lauded research in the social sciences, particularly in the study of suicide and serious mental disorders. I was deeply involved in the construction of chishiki. I felt satisfaction in contributing in a small way to the further intellectual understanding of human thought and behavior, but I felt some dissatisfaction, too. For whenever I got enough control over the data to be able to say something definite scientifically, the situation was so artificial that the data were meaningless outside of it. In other words, when you put humans in an experimental situation (or even when you get them to answer questionnaires or take psychological tests) you have created such an artificial situation that what they do in the situation may have little to do with what they do outside of it. And when you observe people in their natural, everyday life there are so many variables affecting what they do that it becomes impossible to predict or explain their behavior with any strict scientific accuracy.

Such is the problem with chishiki. The closer we look at a problem, the more we discover that is unclear. And, I believe, the less satisfied we become with chishiki alone as a guide for our lives. We crave something more dependable, more lasting. That something may be chie, wisdom or understanding. Perhaps it is the same as "gut knowledge." I know that what I understand experientially is certain in a way somehow different from what I know intellectually, rationally. Intellectual knowledge sometimes helps me to put a finger on the wisdom that lies in my experience, but the two are never the same. Clear, rational argument may help me change the way I see some intellectual issue, but no amount of clever discourse can change what I understand experientially. There is no need to change the little nibble of wisdom that I understand. It is truth, solid, dependable. When I write, for example, that this constructive lifeway places responsibility for living with each of us (not with spouse or family or society or race), that what we do determines who we are, I write with confidence. Such a statement is true. No amount of argument or scientific experimentation can change the truth value of the statement that what I do determines who I am. Nor is such a statement tautological, or circular. Circular statements cannot be disproved either, but they are merely definitional. "We don't do what we aren't motivated to do" is an example of a circular statement. We discover that someone isn't motivated to do something by watching whether he does that something or not. If he doesn't do it then we assume he wasn't motivated. Then we explain why he didn't do it by saying he wasn't motivated. "What I do" is not the same thing as "who I am." It remains true that what I do determines who I am—no tautology, no disproof. Check it out with your experience.

Interestingly, one of the functions of psychology and other social sciences has been to demonstrate that naïve, commonsense interpretations of human behavior are too simplistic. A concomitant danger, however, has been a bias among most social scientists against any commonsense interpretations of human behavior. One isn't likely to get a degree or advance up the academic ladder by researching and discovering what any layperson seems to know

DAVID K. REYNOLDS

already. A good student asks questions, but doesn't directly challenge his mentor's approach or findings. A student with potential in the social sciences forms an attachment to a well-known researcher and pushes along in the wake of chishiki.

Similarly, unless a psychotherapist appears to have some expert, arcane knowledge and skill there seems to be no advantage to talking with a therapist over talking with a friend. The therapist, like the academic social scientist, must appear to be in possession of special knowledge that is deep and difficult for laypeople to understand. The corresponding role for the "patient" in traditional psychotherapy is to remain a sort of trusting child. The patient learns the mystical interpretation of his "illness" or problem as taught by the therapist. As a social child the patient is protected by ethics and the law from the therapist's power and sexual interest, just as a child is protected from adults. During therapy there is often elaborate maneuvering aimed at keeping the patient childlike, without responsibility for behavior. In legal matters, too, the person in therapy or in need of therapy is considered to be lacking in responsibility for what he does. Therapist and patient collude to maintain this aura of mysterious probing into some equally mysterious psyche. Sometimes the results are as hoped for, sometimes not.

Yet problems of the psyche are simplified considerably when adults accept adult responsibility for what they do. The reasons why we do what we do, how we receive the ability and privilege to be able to do what we do, how and why we choose what needs doing, and so forth are dimensions underlying this adult responsibility. To be candid, no one knows much about these dimensions. Let me state the facts plainly: No one has a clear understanding of why we do or think or feel as we do. We would like to believe that our anxiety is due to an unresolved Oedipus complex or an uncaring mother or a malfunctioning neurotransmitter in the brain or the stress at work or some other simple explanation. If we could believe in some simple explanation then perhaps we could do something about the cause and free ourselves from anxiety or any other troubling problem. In fact, *no one knows*. Isn't it more honest and straightforward, then, to admit that chishiki won't (at least now and perhaps ever) save us, and get on about our lives? The truly skilled therapist relies more on chie than on chishiki when engaged in the practice of psychotherapy.

A major goal of this book is to direct our thinking toward some of the ways in which understanding affects behavior and feelings.

Mirrors

I remember as a child sitting on the padded board laid across the arms of a sturdy metal barber's chair. I could see my face reflected in the mirror, and the reflection of the reflection, and the reflection of the reflection of the reflection. Each reflection bouncing off the mirrors in front and behind distorted the image ever so slightly until it dipped out of sight.

Neurosis is rather like watching reflections in barber shop mirrors. There is nothing really wrong with my clients just as they are. But they are obsessed with *(torawarete iru,* in Japanese, "caught by") their distorted views of themselves. As the Zen people would put it, they already are Buddhas; they don't need some special enlightenment. But they don't recognize who they are and what they have already. So they come for "treatment" or "guidance" or "training" to be relieved of their suffering.

In their reflected images they see themselves as hurting more than other people, interfering with and interfered with in their movement toward success and happiness. They *are* unnecessarily miserable, but the fault lies not in themselves, and not even in their upbringing or in more recent tragedies. The problem lies in the images they create, images of how life ought to be, what might have been, who they should be instead of who they are.

If they insist on being obsessed with reflections I advise them to follow the infinity of reflections wholeheartedly until they become tired of the progressive distortion. For example, if they criticize themselves, I ask them to criticize their criticisms of themselves, and then to criticize themselves criticizing their self-criticism. Why do they have confidence in their self-doubts? Why not doubt their self-doubts? And doubt themselves doubting their doubts about themselves? And so on. There is merit in lacking confidence in their own lack of confidence. My students simply aren't neurotic enough. They follow the images partway and then stop, believing them. To follow the reflections on and on reveals their absurd distortions.

The reality of me is just me.

Heroic Vision

I suppose to some people the sort of acceptance of reality proposed by our way of constructive living seems unnecessarily tough. It certainly is·pragmatic and realistic, but there is no promise of continuous joy, no hope of a constant high. I know of no one who stays joyful all of the time. Perhaps it would be easy to live life fully if our existence always moved along pleasantly with satisfying smoothness. The truth is that it doesn't. Phones don't always ring at convenient times; publishers don't adopt my timetable for getting books into print; my clients don't always progress as rapidly as I hope; a supporter sometimes fails to follow through on a promise; my stomach rebels; machines break down; I miss a deadline, fail to meet the needs of a client. Such small disasters certainly aren't the whole of reality, but they are undeniably a part of it.

The heroic vision, it seems to me, is the possibility of living responsively, responsibly in spite of these inconveniences and tragedies. They are, after all, only conditions that reality presents for my consideration and response. I may label them "impassable barriers," "insurmountable obstacles," "irreparable damage," or "unconquerable handicaps," but they don't arrive from reality with such labels already attached. The heroic possibility is that we can build character that takes life's disasters and successes in stride.

There is no doubt about it, suffering will continue to present itself in our lives whatever course we choose to follow. If we can't always be in control of what reality brings, if we can't govern what our feelings are in response to what reality brings, we can, nevertheless, take active control of what we do in response to what reality brings. Therein lies our freedom; therein lies the need for self-discipline in our behavior. We develop the control over our actions by exercising control over our actions again and again. This self-control is our heroic practice. Taking charge of what I do frees me from being the puppet of circumstances or the pawn of my feelings. It offers a path to transcendence.

There are two loci of hope in constructive living. They are indicated by the maxims "Many me's" and "Every moment a fresh one" found in the book *Constructive Living*. The notion of "Many me's" is that we are all changeable. No one is locked into a single personality. We are different from one situation to the next, from one moment to the next.

The way we develop our experiential recognition of the "Many me's" concept is by varying our behavior. Always in constructive living we begin with the area of life where we have the most leverage, our own behavior. By changing what we do we bring out the multiple possibilities of our many selves. Try varying where you eat, how you eat, what you eat. Set your table on the living-room coffee table, have a picnic in the den, try a restaurant with a kind of cuisine you have never tasted. Use your left hand as much as possible for at least an entire day. Dress differently. Change your habits of talking, try out an accent or a change of pace in your speech and tone on a salesperson. Take up a new sport or hobby. Vary what you do in order to verify that you have many more selves than you have developed before. We are all multipossible creations. To see ourselves as only reserved or always shy or bad-tempered or helpless or dependent or generous or wise or anything at all is to define ourselves too narrowly. There are many me's.

"Every moment a fresh one" offers a complementary sort of hope. Reality keeps bringing us fresh moments with which to work, to live our lives. No matter what failure I have experienced in the past, no matter what terrible things I have done, no matter what ingratitude or loss or slap in the face, this present moment reveals itself to me fresh and uncluttered by the past. This moment called now simply presents itself and awaits what I shall do before moving itself along into the past. It appears in its pure neutrality, allowing me any change in my action of which I am physically capable. I can begin building my life in some new direction at any time, merely by taking advantage of this fresh new moment of the now.

Leaving No Footprints

There is a feeling of lightness when we discover that there is no need to stay stuck in old ways of seeing ourselves and the others with whom we live our daily lives. There is no need to stay stuck in old habits and perspectives. We can change it all simply by changing what we do. By changing what I do I change who I am and I change who the others are around me.

Carl decided to give some of the cookies he had baked to Hilary, a woman who worked under his supervision. In the giving he discovered that he hadn't been nurturing Hilary as he thought he had in the past. In the giving he found his freedom to see Hilary in a new light—he need not carry with him old prejudices, old views of his righteousness and her pride. In the giving he changed both Carl and Hilary.

How wonderful to be free to choose the direction of our changing! Simply in the doing . . .

Adolescence continues into the late twenties and early thirties these days in our culture. It is in the thirties that many begin to see their parents as fellow humans, their family histories as worth discovering, their cultural roots as worth preserving. One young trainee decides to turn his father into a wise old man. He performs this feat by asking his father's advice on important matters, by seeking his father's wisdom and responding to it, by listening with attention to what his father has to say. He changes himself in the process. But he changes not only his seeing; he changes his father, as well . . . truly. His father becomes a wise old man.

How can I let you grow? How can I let you love? What can I do to stand you on my shoulders to see over the walls of your vision? And from the top of the wall you reach back down to pull me up beside you. It isn't in the hoping. It isn't in the wishing the best for you. It is in the doings large and small. No, there are no small doings. It is in the apology for my lateness, in the carefully selected gifts, in the unsung services of dishwashing and serving your favorite foods and hearing your strength through the complaints. It is in seeing the perfect you as you are, and still supporting the greater perfection of the you you want to become. It is in letters and courtesies and investing my time in you, letting you select the course of our strolling.

How free it feels to follow you—for your/my/our sake.

Revealing the Hidden Agenda

The reality is that the legal system is set up for the convenience of the judges; hospitals and universities are organized for the convenience of the administration. However much those in power talk about serving their constituents, there is little evidence of anything but token concern for citizens, patients, students. The institutions of religion and politics now serve those in authority; big business serves big capital; few of us choose to serve one another.

The scholar becomes more and more divorced from studies of how to live meaningfully, effectively. Teachers teach little that is of value in becoming fully human. Few even remember how to see through the lies, the attempts to impress, the advertised hypocrisy. It is all such a bother. Simpler just to drop into the pharmacies and liquor stores to have the prescriptions filled; simpler to forget, to ignore, to pretend.

Somewhere along our historical line we began to confuse honesty about feelings with acting on feelings. Sometime we began to see self-discipline as old-fashioned and out of place in a world of abundance. We began to make economics the measure of all things, even in our social sciences, in our marriages, in our dreams for our children. Perhaps we expected our churches and schools and family life to keep us from straying from the values that hacked a world power out of tough lands and tough peoples.

urches were caught in dream worlds of words and feel-
d our schools were drifting aimlessly under self-seeking
istrators, and parents were perplexed by change and se-
ced by extrafamilial pastimes. There came a time when most
people worked only to make money, to get themselves ahead, to
achieve economic security in a narrow self-interested sense.

We drifted into hot wars and cold wars and the lying-bribing-
stupidity called "intelligence" operations. We stood only for the
principle of expedience and left the running of the world to big
business, big military, big politics. Perhaps we thought naïvely that
they would leave the rest of us alone in exchange for their power.
But young men died in wars and on streets with heroin needles in
their arms. Young women poisoned their babies with drugs touted
by big business and big medicine. Young people dropped out then
drifted back, disillusioned with retreat, with politics, with a straight
life. Back to looking out for me, number one, avoiding burnout,
getting the most for the least. Giveaway programs, lotteries, prize-
o-grams, the old something-for-nothing illusions hold the flags
many follow these days. These empty contest-winners are our
heroes-for-a-moment.

It has to change. We have to change. We have to see that it is
the earning that counts and not merely what is earned. We have to
put the chance of winning at life back in the hands of each of us
and not in the hands of the rich and the powerful alone.

I have been trying to teach my students to see that respect is
due a person because of the way in which he or she does what
needs doing rather than because of the person's position or social
status, wealth or fame. It happens that what needed to be done for
some people led to current power and recognition in government,
business, the military, the arts, and so forth. It is the way in which
they conduct their current activities, the quality of their moment-
by-moment doing that makes some of them worthy of our respect.
Respect must be continually earned. The distinction between who
we are (being) and what we do (doing) is an artificial one. We are
what we do.

Constructive living aims at nothing less than setting a country back on its meaningful path. The methods are the meanest and most inefficient imaginable. They aim at changing people one by one. How naïve! And yet, how else? New laws merely lead to deeper sophistication in lawbreaking and more business for lawyers. Religious pronouncements produce words and talk about words and definitions of talk about words. Academic studies offer statistical tabulations of what image-encrusted officials in government and other funding agencies are doodling about in their minds this year.

Perhaps it makes some sense to seek our way back to self-discipline, responsibility, courageous pioneering, and seeing beyond self-interest on a person-by-person basis. I may not influence many, but those who give this lifeway a serious try will *know* its depth without statutes or commandments or statistics. There is nothing so solidly convincing as personal experience.

On Being Natural

When we say that the weather is terrible or that it is a pleasant day we are really talking about our convenience and our preference and not about some moral quality of the weather. The weather just is. It is cloudy or drizzly or foggy or clear or nippy or whatever. It is what nature presents to us at a particular time. We must take the weather into account when we dress to go out in it, when we plan a picnic, when we decide what tires to put on the car, when we decide whether to carry an umbrella to work. Nevertheless, the weather doesn't force us to make any particular decision about what we shall do. For example, we may choose to wear a swimsuit in the rain and wash our car in a drizzle, we may continue with our picnic plans even though it is windy, we may decide that snow tires are too expensive to buy, and we may prefer to run to the car rather than use an umbrella.

The weather is part of the natural reality that is presented to us for our consideration. So are feelings. Being afraid of heights is just as natural as a breezy autumn day; so is nervousness when we are about to meet new and important people in our lives. Anxiety before taking an examination, concern while waiting for medical laboratory reports on our physical condition, embarrassment when we have made a blunder in front of others, grief when a loved one (or a job) is lost—all these feelings are as natural as the weather.

When we try to single out some feelings as "terrible" or "un-warranted" or "intrusive" or "hindering" or "beneath us," we are likely to forget their proper naturalness. When we recognize their essential innocence we can go on about life, simply acknowledging their existence as we acknowledge a foggy morning. It is sensible to try to work our way around fog—we use dimmed headlights, drive slower, and so forth. Anyone who tries to attack the fog directly seems foolish to us. It does no good to slash away at fog with a sword or a fan. Why, then, do we try to get rid of our fears and anxieties? Why is the purpose of some psychotherapies to try to free the patients from worries and self-doubts and apprehensions? I suspect that some therapists try this impossible task not only because their patients are distressed by their feelings (some people are distressed by gloomy weather, too), but also because the therapists and patients have the mistaken notion that the feelings somehow interfere with the patients' doing what they need to do in life.

We commonly say, for example, that Mr. X won't fly on an airplane because he is afraid of flying. We may even believe that Mr. X's fear causes him to refrain from flying. It isn't so. It can't be so, because there are plenty of people who fear flying (I am one of them) and yet travel by plane all the time. Perhaps, you say, it is the degree of fear that distinguishes between people who fly and people who don't. I wonder. I used to be very, very frightened (much more than I am now) and still flew because there was no other reasonable way to get from Los Angeles to Japan and back in the time available.

In the psychology of suicide we often talk about persons who are too depressed to be suicidal. The danger of suicide comes when their depression begins to lift. While they are at the bottom of depression they have no energy to plan or act on their suicidal plan. So it is not the feeling of depression that causes people to kill themselves. Throughout human life, it is simply impossible to make a clear, simple causal connection between what we feel and what we do. When we look closely at feelings and behavior we see some correlation (like the correlation between the number of

DAVID K. REYNOLDS

umbrellas we see on the street and rainclouds in the sky) but no simple causal relationship (just as we see some people without umbrellas even though it is raining).

I do not know what causes us to do what we do. I really don't. I know that it isn't simply feelings. I suspect that no one else is certain about what causes us to act as we do, either, although some claim such awesome insight. It seems clear, however, that when we get to the point of accepting our feelings as we accept the inevitability of the weather, when we take into consideration the information about our feelings as we consider the information in a weather report, and then go ahead with what we have decided needs to be done, we end up in better shape than those who shake their fists at the clouds in the sky or scream at (or ignore) the weather reports.

You see, even the most unpleasant feelings are the natural result of our wanting to live and to live fully. The fear of meeting others grows from the desire to be liked and respected by them. The fear of heights is self-preserving, reflecting a reluctance to put ourselves in dangerous situations. Self-criticism and feelings of inferiority indicate a strong desire to improve ourselves. We compare ourselves with real or imagined others, noticing their apparent abilities and successes. Our skill at observation and our strong drive to succeed are reflected in our self-doubts. People who don't care about living successfully don't have worries about job interviews and examinations; they don't have inferiority feelings; they don't suffer from shyness or lack of confidence. Those who don't care are to be pitied.

If we grow beyond the petty human feelings and concerns then we lose empathy and sympathy for other suffering humans. It is far better to continue to feel while developing better discipline in our behavior. In this way, we don't lose our membership in humanity, though we advance up the ranks of character.

The "natural" person, then, simply takes the feelings as they come, all intertwined and interacting, and goes about doing what reality brings that needs doing. The "natural" person wastes no time trying to struggle with feelings directly. The feelings are just "ordinary," unworthy of lots of attention over a long period of time. Feelings shouldn't be ignored—how could we ignore a snowstorm, anyway?—but when you have to go out in a blizzard, you go out. That is the way it is to be human. The feelings are there, but we do what we have to do. Even in summer, when the ice hasn't melted, shivering, we do what we have to do.

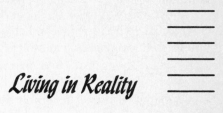

Living in Reality

"I have no pleasure in life."
  "How does that cola taste?"

"I put myself in positions where I just can't—"
  "Let's talk about what you need to do this afternoon."

"I've always had this desire to break through the ordinary, to go beyond—"
  "Your shoe is untied."

"Why is it that I never seem to be able to nourish others?"
  "What did you have for lunch today?"

"The damn lawyer never gets anything right. I'm always in some mess like this. Absolute chaos!"
  "Do you notice that you use words like 'never' and 'always' and 'absolute' a lot?"

"I didn't sleep all night."
  "What time was on the clock when you were awake? What did you do?"

"When we have these altercations I feel the need to ventilate. There's this cathartic response, you know, when I download the aggression."

"During the fight yesterday how did you show your anger? What did you do?"

"I was born with this introverted character. Nothing I do seems to change it. During junior and senior high school I suffered terribly . . . alone . . . isolated. Now, in college, the same pattern continues."

"We'll leave your introversion as it is for the moment. What classes are you taking this semester? What clubs have you joined? Who do you study with?"

"All last week I felt—"

"How did you feel as you walked into the office just now? What were you doing just then?"

"My attitude even shows at work."

"How does it show? When was the last time it showed? What did you do then?"

"I usually brush my teeth, then rinse out my mouth, dry my face . . . then, uh, I walk out of the bathroom. . . ."

"Not 'usually'—'This morning I brushed my teeth.' What hand did you use to hold the toothpaste this morning? Which hand unscrewed the cap? Where was the toothbrush while you were opening the toothpaste? Which hand reached for the towel to dry your face? How did the floor of the bathroom feel on your feet this morning?"

"I just wasn't motivated to write in the journal."

"You mean you didn't write in it."

"That's what I said."

"No, you said that you weren't motivated to write in the journal."

"That's why I didn't write in it."

"When you do something, you were motivated to do it; when you don't do something, you weren't motivated to do it. What does 'motivation' add as an explanation? The reality is that you didn't write in it."

"It's so hard to go on. . . ." (Sobs.)
"Here, have a tissue."

"When we argue I try to listen patiently."
"You listen or you don't, moment by moment. Patience is a feeling, and so it is uncontrollable. When you are patient, be patient; when you aren't patient, accept that state, too. Keep listening anyway."

"We are working on developing a communicative relationship."
"What is a 'communicative relationship'? What do you do in one? When was the last time you had one? What were you doing then? Do we have one right now? How does one work on developing a 'communicative relationship'? What do we need to do now in order to develop one?"

"After all, I have choices."
"Name some."
"I think I'm going to try to learn to relate better."
"When? How? Tell me exactly what you plan to do."

"There seem to be some underlying resistances to that assignment. I explored my associations to buying her a gift and found some hidden resentment about—"
"You didn't buy her the gift. Shall we move on to another assignment? Do you need to get the gift, resentment or not?"

"I just don't seem to have time to do what I know needs to be done."
"Let's take a look at yesterday. What time did you get up? Then what did you do?"

"I have to get my intention up on it."
   "No, just do it."
   "All right, I'll make more of a commitment."
   "No, just do it."

"I want instant answers, instant insights. There's so much I want to do with my life."
   "Give me an example of something you want to do today."

"How do I know what needs to be done?"
   "Ask the situation."

"I keep discovering how unaware I am."
   "The more aware you become, the more you notice your lack of awareness."

"I seem to be unwilling to do it."
   "You mean, that you haven't done it."

"I'm very good at setting goals, but not at all good at achieving them."
   "There is a difference between setting goals as an intellectual task and finding what needs to be done in this moment."

"I'm worried that I may have cancer."
   "What have you done to find out?"
   "Nothing, but I feel this swelling."
   "What needs to be done? When? What needs to be done while waiting for the tests and results?"

"I need to go out and meet people."
   "How are you going to start? What can you do today about this goal?"

"I'm a child because I'm behaving like a child and she treats me like a child."

"You're not a child."

"I do everything I can for him, but he doesn't seem to appreciate it."
"Let's consider what is controllable and what isn't. Then we'll talk about your purposes in serving him."

"I'm having this problem with overeating. I need to get myself together. If I could just get it all together . . ."
"No, you need to stop eating so much and to exercise more."
"But I'm nervous and that makes me hungry all the time."
"What is the difference between being hungry and eating?"

"I can't remember what I did this morning."
"We'll wait for a while until something comes to you."

"Therapy has helped me be more in control of my feelings."
"Feelings are uncontrollable; behavior is controllable."

"I resist making those telephone calls."
"Yes, you feel that resistance *and* you make those calls."

"I'm not worth anything."
"Are you supporting your wife and children?"
"Yes."
"Have you started your own business in tough econmoic times?"
"Yes."
"Are you working steadily at it?"
"Yes."
"Didn't you say you sent your mother a Christmas card and gift?"
"Yes."
"You're working every day on a self-development program?"
"Yes."
"While feeling worthless keep on being useful. The feelings will change if you keep the behavior purposeful and constructive."

"I seem to be confronting all these major issues at once."

"Did you notice that your car is parked with the headlights still on?"

"I'm so insecure. If only I had the confidence to try designing."

"Insecurity is fine. Confidence will come after you succeed at designing, not before. While feeling insecure, while lacking in confidence, do what needs to be done."

"I feel anxious all the time."

"Do you feel anxious now?"

"Yes."

"Close your eyes, please. What is the color of the rug in this room? What is the color of the drapes?"

"I don't know."

"Describe the clothing I am wearing."

"Hmmmm, I didn't notice."

"Where is your anxiety right now? Oh, here it comes again."

DAVID K. REYNOLDS

Remaking the Past

We are continuously creating our histories. What I do now will be filed away in tomorrow's past. Once this now has become part of my past it cannot be changed—its successes cannot be taken away from me; its excesses cannot be erased. Constructive living works to create a past that is filled with purposeful, meaningful activity. With such a past I become one-who-lives-constructively.

For it is our history that determines who we are now. I evaluate myself in terms of what has been my history. If I am one who ran away from troubles in the past then I see myself as a coward; if I am one who sacrificed for my principles then I am a principled person. Fortunately, we have the ability to create a new past by means of changing what we are doing now. This moment becomes the recent past. Then it begins to sink beneath the weight of even more recent events, like sediment on the floor of the ocean. The old floor of my past can be completely covered by layers of new behaviors and habits.

It is important to emphasize that the past doesn't determine what we do now. Rather, we determine what the past will become by what we do now. The way I handle a problem now need have no relationship with the way I handled a similar problem in the past. I can change who I am by trying new solutions to recurring problems, by tucking old behaviors safely into the past.

Public Misconceptions

A recent magazine ad reads:

"Barbara's problem isn't her weight. Her weight is only a symptom. A symptom of a serious illness. She's physically addicted to food and psychologically obsessed with it.

"She doesn't need more diets. She needs professional medical care. . . ."

It is hard to accept the idea that anyone could believe such foolishness. Barbara's problem *is* her weight. Better yet, the photograph shows that Barbara is fat. Barbara is better off facing the reality that confronts her than hiding behind some ludicrous pseudomedical label of illness. She may have other problems, too, of course. But to attempt to define them all as medical problems is to make all of life medical. She *does* need a diet, and exercise. She needs to change what she eats and how much she eats and, probably, when she eats. Her problem of overweight is no more medical than the problem of laziness or pessimism or criminality.

We are all "physically addicted to food." We had better be if we wish to stay alive. We all become psychologically obsessed with food when we haven't eaten for a long while. Barbara's problem is neither addiction nor obsession. She eats too much; she exercises too little or improperly. Let's be realistic.

Alcoholism, too, has come to be mislabeled as illness by

some, as has neurosis. I wait for the ad programs that will promote a treatment for the "illness of jealousy," or "Cure bad penmanship medically!" or "Enter Lawngreen Hospital and overcome your laziness." It is all too easy to sidestep responsibility for what we do by labeling our problem an illness, a medical problem. But it is sheer absurdity.

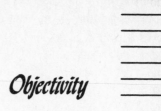

Objectivity

Morita therapy and Naikan share a characteristic attitude toward objective observation. In areas with strong emotional impact both of these therapies ask the client to observe in detail what is occurring, rather as a naturalist would observe the behavior of wild geese or insects. In one Moritist hospital in Japan this naturalistic observation is carried to the point that patients spend hours studying ladybugs and recording their observations in journals.

What is involved here is more than mere infatuation with an aspect of the scientific method. There is no need to generate emotion during therapy, no need to encourage the expression of gratitude or guilt during Naikan reflection on how much others did for us in the past and how little we returned to them, for example. The looking itself is sufficient. Underlying this procedure is a valuing of awareness much like that in psychoanalysis. But in Freudian thought the awareness should lead to a diminishing of emotion-laden symptoms. In Morita therapy and Naikan the awareness is an end in itself. Even when it provokes feelings of despair (as when the patient reviews a miserable past during bed rest in Morita therapy) and remorse (for example, during the review of one's mistreatment of others in Naikan) the observation in itself is good, and it must continue in spite of the feelings it generates.

The feelings that well up during self-observation are not problems. Feelings are never really problems in themselves. When they are accepted as they are *(arugamama ni* [Morita], *sunao ni* [Naikan]) they are simply more data to be observed, providing information about but not determination of what needs to be done.

In our neurotic moments we forget to observe. We become overwhelmed by feelings of anger, depression, jealousy, embarrassment, and the like. As these feelings happen to us we fail to maintain an active stance of observing and defining them. We fail to keep an eye on the reality that is presenting us with something to be done in this moment. If you are bickering with your spouse (or parent) as he or she drives you to work (or school), the driver still deserves a word of thanks for the effort of driving. The anger doesn't relieve you of the responsibility to credit the other person's effort in your behalf. A genuine understanding of this point puts emotions in their proper place. For obvious artistic reasons, dramatic entertainment in plays, films, and novels has inflated the importance of emotion all out of proportion to its necessary effect on our lives. Feelings are no more than spice for the main course of our existence—what we do.

Purpose

One of the fundamental principles of this constructive lifeway is to know one's purpose. When a moment's purpose is clear we can move directly toward accomplishing it. Some people seem to have no guiding purposes that offer broad direction to their moment-by-moment purposes. They seem scattered, impulsive, with no long-term goals. Such people need an experience that creates life goals and purposes for living. Naikan is an effective method for many of these people.

It is relatively easy to determine the topics of a client's Naikan self-reflection. Every client complains about certain people and situations in life. Those complaints and criticisms that are strong and continuing point toward appropriate topics for Naikan. They reflect an inability or unwillingness to perceive the contributions of these other people and situations in the client's life. Naikan forces the clients to see the side of reality that they have consistently ignored. In steadily viewing the positive contributions of friends and enemies alike, a natural desire to serve and repay is generated in the majority of clients. Such a goal provides the life direction and order to immediate purposes so that Morita's method can be effective.

We may assign a journal in which the client is to keep track of momentary purposes. This assignment is made in order to help the client keep clear on the purposes that are guiding behavior. Such journals also give us an indication of problems that are ocurring in the area of purpose. For example, the purposes "to have a nice birthday" and "to enjoy myself today" are too vague, too general, and uncontrollable. When a child is ill the purpose "to make my child well" is beyond my power, but the purposes "to take my child for treatment," "to sponge her forehead when the fever rises," and "to call the doctor" are much more practical. Clients who characteristically set goals that they have little chance of reaching will understandably be disappointed and dissatisfied with much of life. Clients with goals that are so vague and general that it is difficult to tell whether the goals have been reached are likely to be timid, because they are not building confidence on a succession of clear accomplishments.

Another variant of the journal asks the client to write immediate purposes on one side of a page and, alongside on the same page, what actions were carried out to achieve the purposes. This format helps the client to see the immediate connection between a goal and the action necessary to reach it. Even the simplest act may have many purposes behind it. The deeper one looks at purpose, the more introspectively analytic and subjective becomes the process. There is no need to carry such self-analysis too far. It can become merely another escape from doing what needs to be done in our daily lives, an escape from constructive but difficult action. There is need for a careful balance between self-examination and forthright action. If either side of that balance is neglected, destructive results become likely.

It is useful for us to examine our purposes in examining our purposes, too. That is, what do we expect to achieve by becoming clear about our purposes? Are we engaged in an intellectual exercise, a process of self-discovery, a step toward more fulfilling action, some combination or none of these possibilities?

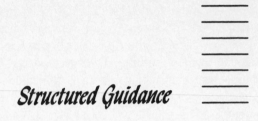

Structured Guidance

A VARIETY OF HARMONIOUS TECHNIQUES.

Psychotherapy is not magical. It is not necessarily deeper or more elegant a process than counseling, guidance, personal management training, individualized education, or a good talk with a wise friend. One difference is that psychotherapists must be licensed in order to call themselves psychotherapists in their states, and they may charge more than some professional helpers, but often less than psychiatrists (who are medical doctors and can prescribe medication).

In the constructive living guidance that is sometimes called Morita therapy or Morita training or the Morita method or simply "playing ball," we use a variety of techniques to achieve the goals of personal growth and increased human maturity. Fortunately, a person need not be neurotic to benefit from learning this lifeway. The dissatisfaction and unhappiness that we call neurotic is no different in quality from the misery that we all feel in some moments of our lives. In this chapter we consider the elements of our life training and how they fit together into a single coordinated package for the client's development. There is much more offered the client than a listening ear. Training includes personalized teaching, experiential homework assignments, reading assignments, life scheduling, and a living model (embodied in the thera-pist/guide) of the therapeutic concepts, in addition to the trained listening that most therapies and self-management programs have to offer.

ONE SIZE DOESN'T FIT ALL

Good teaching is geared toward the needs of the individual client. However, each client shares some qualities with all humans so that some of our teaching applies to everyone we see. For exam-ple, no one is capable of controlling feelings directly by the will. All of us experience the fading of feelings over time unless we restimulate them with our behavior or our circumstances. No one remains aware of the pumping of the heart or the blinking of the eyes at all times. No one can predict or control the emergence of thoughts into consciousness with any consistency. No one's suffer-ing is so unique that others cannot have some degree of under-standing of and empathy with it, however imperfect. We share similar psychological mechanisms of defense, of simplification, of constant change, of selective attention, of reciprocal interaction. We all grow old if we survive long enough; we know sorrow, abandonment, pleasure; we shall all know death.

Good teaching finds a way to demonstrate the general princi-ples in the particular life of the student. It looks to the student's circumstances to find examples and problem areas and models and solutions. It doesn't get caught in the trap of taking respon-sibility for the student's learning, for that is the student's job. But good teaching keeps track of where the student is and measures out the lessons accordingly.

Perhaps a third of each hourly session with every student (held at least once each week) is devoted to teaching. The student may have questions from the readings and experiential assignments de-scribed below. Questions are one indication to the guide of what needs to be taught. Questions often represent an emptiness in the client's mind ready for filling and subsequent digestion. Or, like the overflowing teacup, a client's mind may have no room left for pouring in new information at some times.

A number of constructive activities are designed to carry the teaching and experience of this lifeway beyond the hourly sessions. Our students live 168 hours during a week; if our training is to have maximal impact we cannot expect it all to be accomplished in a single hour.

The readings that I assign are of several kinds. Of course, there are readings about Morita therapy. Much of what is written about Morita therapy in English is presented in the same conversational style as in this book. The illustrations and principles are presented in an easily understood format, often in the form of stories and maxims. The students find such readings helpful reminders of what they are learning directly from their guide and what they are practicing daily in their lives. The reading assignments are no substitute for direct teaching or experiential exercises. But they satisfy the students' hunger for intellectual knowledge about their practice.

Another kind of reading assignment is fitted to the particular needs of each student. When the students lack knowledge about areas important in their lives they are encouraged to read up on those areas. When they have doubts about their abilities as parents they may be assigned library trips to gather materials on parenting skills. When they are concerned about dysfunctions of their bodies they may be assigned popular medical texts to read. Why make decisions on the basis of imagination when there is reliable information available in print?

Part of character development involves a broadening of awareness and interest in the world about us. Readings in psychology, anthropology, biography, sports, gardening, travel, and so forth help to expand the student's horizons beyond a narrow self-focus. A person with a variety of interests can take a blow in one area with more equanimity than someone whose only preoccupation is his or her own business activity, for example.

EXPERIENTIAL EXERCISES

Assignments to visit art exhibits, listen to a variety of musical styles, and attend adult education classes have broadening functions. As experiential explorations mount, more and more information is accumulated about reality. It is axiomatic in constructive life guidance that acting on reality brings more trustworthy information about the real world than imagination alone. We are what we do. So the emphasis is on changing and expanding the doing in order to change who we are. The experiential exercises are designed to help the clients do love, do courage, do appreciation, do studying, do giving, do serving, do exploration *no matter what they are feeling*. Gradually, they come to see that in the doing, their feelings are likely to change. And, in any event, the feelings become less insistent, although they remain noticed and accepted elements of experience.

So the experiential assignments might include saying a minimal number of "thank you" and "I'm sorry" statements each day (again, whether or not the client actually feels grateful or repentent). There might be an assignment to pick up trash in a nearby park or telephone a friend of years gone by or call for a job interview or write a journal about sounds heard during the day. Taking a gift to a rival, acknowledging a parent's contribution to our upbringing by writing a letter describing some concrete event in which the parent sacrificed for us but never received a word of thanks since then, offering time as a volunteer in a nursing care facility or a playground, doing an unannounced service for someone, giving a new hobby or a new cooking style a try—any of these exercises will teach us something about reality, and about ourselves as part of that reality.

Morita, the wise Japanese psychiatrist who formulated many of the principles of this lifeway nearly seventy years ago, recognized that intellectual understanding is not the same as experiential understanding. Reading about reality alone is insufficient. Furthermore, however much we understand with our intellects, our emotional attachments are quite another thing. Morita wrote that people know that milk is likely to promote good health and liquor is not, but that doesn't mean that everyone likes milk and avoids liquor. Clear logical arguments and good solid advice won't do the trick. If our students won't give this lifeway an experiential try, the information they hear and read will not be maximally useful to them.

THE ORGANIZED LIFE

How can one expect to have an orderly mind while living in a disorderly lifestyle? If we truly are what we do, then it is no wonder that anxiety and self-doubt usually accompany poor habits of living in even the most basic human functions of eating, sleeping, and exercise.

In Tokyo, Morita had read of Ludwig Binswanger's five-week course in regulated living as practiced in Germany. Morita perceived that the organization of daily life was an important element in clearing a student's mind, so he adapted some elements of Binswanger's method. However, the European's emphasis was on rest and scheduling the patient's life in the hospital so that medical treatment could be facilitated. Morita saw that neurotic problems aren't really illness, so he changed the scheduling emphasis from medical treatments to the student's own work and study. And he moved the treatment program out of the hospital and into his own home. Nowadays, we help our clients to organize their lives in their own homes and at their own places of work and play.

A recent issue of one Morita therapy magazine from Japan contains a description of the order one student of this lifestyle chose to impose on his life. Mr. Katsuyama wrote of his plan to get up at 5:30 A.M. and go to bed at 11 P.M. each day. His plan included the resolution to leave work behind when he leaves the office, talk more with his wife, spend more time with his children (providing more experiential learning experiences for them and being more of a model father to them), take courses and increase reading to develop his skills at the bank where he works, pursue concrete plans preparing him for retirement, lend a helping hand to those at

work who have been beaten down by the competitive atmo-
sphere, develop two hobbies (an outside physical pursuit, hiking
in nature; and a stress-relieving inside pursuit, classical singing),
work on listening to others more, make friends at work and in
Morita groups and in conjunction with his hobbies and classes,
practice some form of meditation, pursue some study of religious
matters, and broaden his base of interests and activities.

Each of Mr. Katsuyama's goals could be broken down into
more specific activities. Flexible plans for the day based on general goals are developed in our training sessions in the United
States. Sometimes a list of things that need doing in the next few
days is created during our weekly session and checked off as each
task if accomplished.

We cannot be rigid about structuring a daily plan of activities.
Reality doesn't always allow us to carry out our plans to completion in precisely the time and order we desire. But some plan of
action is a good guideline for keeping us focused on our purpose.
And a list allows us to see our progress as each item is checked
off. To face all our obligations at once may be overwhelming; to
try to keep all of what needs doing in memory may be taxing and
distracting from the immediate pursuit at hand. A schedule and a
list help put a measured order to our day. They offer us some
perspective. But they provide no substitute for *action* on our purposes.

THE GUIDE AS MODEL

An ice-thawing guide must live this lifeway as well as teach it. The
students must be able to see the principles of constructive living in
the conduct of their teachers. That is why I am so selective in the
persons I train and certify to practice these methods. It is also the
reason why our certification programs at the ToDo Institute in Los
Angeles and the Health Center Pacific on Maui include the same
individual sessions and the same experiential exercises and life
scheduling and assigned reading that the trainees will be using
with their clients in the future.

Sometimes our individual sessions with clients/students take place in supermarkets or while apartment hunting or digging in a garden or cleaning a kitchen or traveling or hiking or walking around the block. The practice of these life principles is not restricted to an office. The attention I devote to driving and selecting food items and drying dishes must match the attention I offer my students while listening to them. Getting outside the office helps reinforce the realization that the techniques are useful everywhere, at all times.

EXPEDIENT MEANS

What I emphasize when teaching this constructive manner of living varies from student to student. The advice and exercises vary, too. This flexibility in teaching is based on an inflexible, absolute principle. The principle is that truth only has meaning within a particular situation. There are no truths, no principles that hold irrespective of the context in which they are embedded. Even scientific truths.

A scientific law, for example, is demonstrated within some experimental setting. Provided that the critical elements of the setting are replicated again and again the results of the experiment will be the same again and again. If the results are not duplicated the scientists begin to consider what aspect of the situation was different, and so revise their formulation of the laws under consideration. Alternatively, they may purposely vary certain conditions within the experimental situation to see what sorts of different results are produced by these changes. In any case, the findings are always inextricably tied to experimental conditions or situations in which the scientific observations were made. There are no situation-free truths.

A paradox, you say? "There are no situation-free truths" must depend on some situation, too. I suspect so. Perhaps one situation might be called the limits of human thinking or the nature of the human condition. At any rate, the situational embeddedness of truth seems to hold pretty well across my experience. So it must be reflected in the way I work with my students.

As I walk down the street with Fred during our weekly training session I advise him to keep moving his eyes slowly from side to side in order to scan what reality is bringing him from moment to moment. Fred is depressed and so tied up in himself that he is paying little attention to anything but his own personal and business problems. In contrast, Ed's eyes keep flitting from spot to spot, never resting on any object, never meeting my eyes. Ed appears to be fleeing from some unpleasant reality by shifting his focus about. I advise Ed to fix his gaze upon the flower vase near his chair and to bring it back to the vase whenever he discovers that it has drifted away. The two men received different instructions—expedient means. But the same goal, in the broader sense, and that goal is to use their eyes to affect their thoughts and feelings. We begin with changes of behavior in order to influence our minds.

Recently, I assigned a troubled businessman the extension of words of gratitude and apology to objects as well as people. For weeks his training assignment had been to offer expressions like "thank you" and "I'm sorry" to other people whether he actually felt gratitude and apology or not. As his sensitivity to appropriate situations for these words increased, I added tasks like bowing before his typewriter prior to using it, apologizing to paper before cutting it, thanking the stapler after using it.

Throughout human history there are many precedents for such a custom. Many hunting peoples express regret to game animals before killing them. Agricultural people conduct ceremonies of gratitude to symbolic representatives of their crops. Often anthropologists have interpreted such customs as though the people perceived spirits or gods within plants and animals and tools and rocks and so forth. Whether such interpretations are accurate in every case is questionable; in any case, Western civilization has moved us away from a personal involvement with the objects that surround and serve us day by day. There is much to be said for restoring an appreciation of the service they render us and the lack of proper care we return to them. A calculator performs valuable service, for example. It also represents the labor of inventors and assemblers of components and miners of metal that went into its construction, and salespeople and technicians and many others. It deserves our gratitude and proper care.

There is more than one reason for making the assignment of expressing gratitude and apology to objects. Not only do they merit such behavior because of what they are and what they represent, but the carrying out of the assignment affects the student's view of reality. Compare the businessman who endures work in his office for pay, seeing himself trapped and caged by his job, with the businessman who sees himself surrounded by machines and stock that support him and serve him as companions in the business. The former enters the office and grumbles through the day; the latter greets his office and gives thanks. The former feels isolated; the latter sees himself as part of a mutually supporting team.

Thus, the personal development program employed in this life practice in the United States contains a variety of methods all aimed at helping the students to apply the principles to everyday living. When properly applied the principles do not provide a shield from all pain and suffering (nothing does), but they do offer a life strategy for a richly constructive life, whether pain and suffering are present or not.

Changing Who We Are

Recently, I spoke to a group of patients and ex-patients at a local Veterans Administration psychiatric hospital. One patient would soon be discharged; he was anticipating a return to the same stressful family environment he had been living in when he was admitted to the hospital. He asked for suggestions about minimizing the negative effects of this situation after he returned home. He also wanted to know what to do about the anxiety he felt about leaving the hospital.

There are many parallels to this young man's dilemma in our lives. There are uncomfortable settings and upsetting people we must return to again and again—perhaps at work or at home or in an apartment building or neighborhood or among in-laws. We dread facing them. In a similar way, we hesitate to leave the familiar and comfortable for the unknown. A mental hospital places limits on a patient's rights and freedom, but it soon becomes a place of familiarity and security. Patients make friends with other patients and with staff members. Returning to the lonely, competitive world becomes a frightening step into possible failure.

The constructive advice we can offer a fellow human facing these conditions applies in a variety of related situations. First, if the settings don't change much we must change ourselves in the settings. We change who we are by changing what we do. We remind ourselves to keep on changing what we do by modifying ourselves and the settings as much as possible. For example, I suggested that this young man paint the walls of his room, at least, and rearrange the furniture in his home. He had a beard that he might consider shaving off or he might change his hairstyle or grow a moustache. Different clothes, trying different foods and altered mealtimes, new hobbies and evening study courses, bathing instead of showering or vice versa, a new exercise program, seeking new friends, a different mattress or a sleeping board, different records and musical styles, and so forth could provide reminders that he was different now from when he had gone into the hospital. Always the doing creates the difference in who we are, and it reminds us of that difference. We cannot shovel away our shadows, but we can build more robust bodies so that our shadows are more robust than before.

My recommendation for the anticipatory anxiety he felt about undertaking a life outside the hospital was to go ahead and be anxious. There was nothing to be done about the worry. Chemical tranquilization would just mask a normal fear about the unknown. He ought to have been worried about the step he was taking. The worry showed that he recognized the difficulty of the tasks facing him. The anxiety showed that he wanted to do well on the outside, that he wanted to avoid failure. People who leave the hospital nonchalantly may be walking into difficulties without normal anticipation and preparation.

While the natural stress of the upcoming discharge had to be accepted as it was, the upset could be used to keep this young man actively preparing for the big day. He had to arrange for work on the outside. If he wanted to live away from his family then he must find living accommodations and he must develop the skills of cooking, paying bills, shopping, self-care for minor illness, and the like. As he became involved in preparations and training he would find the anticipatory anxiety somewhat reduced, but it should never go away. Only when he had returned to life outside the hospital and succeeded at it would he have the confidence that he could do it. As usual, confidence follows success.

Advice for Families

Sometimes family members ask what they can do to facilitate their loved one's growth. I tell them the following.

LEARN AND MODEL THE PRINCIPLES

Most important is to learn and model the principles alongside the student. We cannot properly ask a member of our family to make the effort to discipline behavior and accept feelings and hold to purposes if we are unwilling to do so ourselves. The family unit becomes closer as the members work together on a shared path toward the common goal of personal growth. As is discussed in more detail below, changes in one family member are likely to have an effect on others; so the strains put upon the usual family relationships of the past will be better handled if all members can take advantage of these principles of constructive living.

THE PROPER EXPRESSION OF SYMPATHY

It is natural to feel sympathy toward someone who is suffering a great deal. We may also feel anger at the inconvenience the troubled family member is causing us, occasional despair that circumstances will ever improve, envy at the attention he or she receives, and a variety of other feelings. Sympathy is particularly disruptive to the student's growth when we allow it to excuse nonconstructive behavior. As we have stressed again and again, the emphasis of this method is on appropriate action while accepting whatever feelings float through awareness at the time. Students must be encouraged to keep to the tasks they set for themselves even when they are upset by their fears, anxiety, doubts, shyness, rage, sadness, hopelessness, and so forth. The family members must support the constructive behavior through the storms of emotion. In other words, family members, too, must cling to their purpose of being helpful to the student by focusing on action, even though they are being buffeted about by feelings of sympathy and empathy.

At first, this concern with proper action in each moment may be misinterpreted as coolness or lack of caring on the part of others in the family. But it should be made clear to the student by the teacher/guide and by the family that the purpose is to provide encouragement for behavioral change. It is precisely because the family members care so much that they are willing to focus on the necessary changes in behavior that will relieve the student's unnecessary suffering. "I am sad to see you so upset about the term paper that is due on Monday, but you must get to work on it; time is short."

SELF-REVELATION

It is helpful for family members to reveal themselves more to the student. Young people, in particular, may misperceive their parents to be always doing what the parents feel like doing, to be gliding smoothly through life. Parents, in turn, are reluctant to display their weakness and conflicts to their adolescent offspring. Young people need to know that Father doesn't eagerly jump out of bed each morning—that there are mornings when he gets up reluctantly but gets up anyway, knowing that it is his duty to go to work and contribute to the economic support of the family. They need to see that Mother doesn't bring paperwork home from the office because she enjoys doing it, necessarily, but because there is a deadline she is taking the responsibility to meet. Housework

DAVID K. REYNOLDS

isn't always fun. Gardening may be drudgery at times. But part of being a mature adult is "taking care of business" even when not in the mood. Such a capacity sets us apart from young children and animals. They can only respond to and act on their feelings. Adults can choose their behavior within much wider limits.

EXPRESSING GRATITUDE

Supporters of the student should express gratitude and appropriate praise for the behavioral evidence of progress that will appear quite soon in most cases. "It sure is easier for me now that you don't call me to drive up to your dorm every week to help you through a crisis." "Now that you have taken the exam for the promotion we can put it behind us and go out for a fine dinner. Thanks, I'm looking forward to it." "I'm so happy you asked her out. She's such a nice girl." "You haven't gone shopping with me in years. Thanks for bringing me today." "I can talk more openly with you now that you seem so much more together. What a relief for me. Thank you."

Whatever the student's purposes in undertaking training and changing behavior, one result is that a favor is being done the other family members. Life for them becomes easier as the student begins carrying more of a fair share of life's load. Family members become less exhausted thanks to the student's lessened demands for support. So words of gratitude are due the student. They are important both for the student to hear and for the family members to express.

ACCEPTING THE UNCONTROLLABLE

All parents can think of ways they could have raised their children differently, things they should have done, things they shouldn't have done. No parent is perfect. We cannot change what we did in the past. Our past mistakes and successes in parenting are fixed, unalterable. Our responsibility lies only in what we do now. Our chance to affect a spouse or brother or sister or child or parent must be grasped in the present, for the present is all that we have to effect any changes on people in our world, to effect any changes in ourselves. Regret for what might have been in the past merely distracts us from doing well in the present. Accept the past; get on with constructive action right now.

Accept the student as uncontrollable. We aren't responsible for what our family members do. We can encourage and advise them; we can praise and scold them. But, in the end, they do what they do. It is difficult to watch loved ones cause unnecessary pain to themselves and others by their behavior. We do our best to mitigate the unpleasant results of their behavior, but we cannot control them. It is foolish and wasteful to try to do the impossible. The other side of this acceptance of the student's responsibility for the student's behavior is that proper credit goes to the student for constructive changes. We don't want to diminish the self-confidence that follows the student's progress.

Accept your own mixed feelings about changes in the student. There may be a period of rebelliousness or a period of wanting to be isolated from the family or a period of sustained anger at other family members or other reactions. These responses to growth may provoke all sorts of feelings among family members and friends. These feelings are uncontrollable directly by the will. They must be accepted as they are while we go about steadily doing what needs doing. It isn't necessary to feel patient during these turbulent times, it is only necessary to wait.

Similarly, the feelings of helplessness, the frustration at being unable to make perfectly obvious necessary changes in the student, the worrying must be accepted as they are. What else is there to do? These emotional conflicts provide wonderful opportunities for family members to practice and more deeply understand the principles of constructive living in their own lives.

CHANGES WITHIN THE FAMILY

When one family member begins to grow it is likely that there will be some disruption within the family. However troublesome, there was some order and predictability in having everyone behave as usual. When a "neurotic" person starts behaving more "normally," old expectations and behavior patterns of the other people around no longer apply so smoothly. Many people are upset by change. Anger may appear, and jealousy at the attention being focused on the student. Some significant persons in the student's life may express their emotions more freely, having held the expression back in order to protect the frail "neurotic" loved one. As the student displays more control in behavior these significant others may show their resentment at inconveniences and pain caused by the student in the past.

Again, the solution is to wait, while practicing acceptance of feelings and acting purposefully throughout the family. The disruption is minimal when all family members are developing their characters along the same lines with the same method. Fortunately, constructive living principles are useful for everyone who applies them—there is absolutely no stigma that one needs to be "disturbed" or "neurotic" or "ill" or "abnormal" to benefit from them.

DO WHAT YOU CAN

It is important to keep on doing what you can for the student. Be available without pushing or nagging, advise while holding no expectation about whether the student will follow the advice, display the principles of living in your own life. One of our maxims is "Run to the edge of the cliff and stop on a dime." In other words, do all that you can to encourage the student's application of this lifeway into everyday life, but don't get caught up in how successful your efforts are. The efforts alone are sufficient and vital for you and for your loved one.

EXPECT TEMPORARY SETBACKS AND LEARN FROM THEM

Life simply doesn't go as smoothly as it appears in the pages of a book. Progress in constructive living doesn't always proceed neatly in regular fashion. There are big strides of improvement and moments of failure and despair. What is being undertaken, after all, is the reorganization of lives that have muddled along painfully for years in many cases. Habits of thought and behavior must be realigned. For example, after many sessions in which a student seemed to be grasping the principles I've heard, "I'll try not to be upset when I tell my boss I'm resigning, no matter how much he shouts and carries on." Of course, "trying not to be upset" makes no sense. When we are upset, we are. Upset or not, this student must do certain things when resigning. The feelings that arise as the boss "shouts and carries on" are to be noticed and admitted to while the necessary, purposeful behavior is carried out. But the old habits of thinking about and talking about "upset" hadn't been cleared away completely even for this student who had demonstrated remarkable progress over the weeks of her training.

KEEP IN TOUCH WITH THE GUIDE

Although the teacher/guide won't reveal to others what the student talks about during the training sessions, family members will want to keep abreast of general progress and of the experiential homework assignments that the student is working on each week. They may wish to report problems they are encountering and problem areas they believe to be in need of work by the student, or they may have questions about the application of principles in particular circumstances. Sometimes, significant others decide to become students themselves either during or after the course of training of another person in the family. As noted above, positive effects are maximized and disruption minimized when the family cooperates in studying and using these growth principles in every day life.

Ordinary People

The people who come for life management training aren't odd. They don't stand out in a crowd. They do recognize, acutely, that they aren't living up to their potential. They do sense, painfully, life's blows and pressures. On some level they are aware that they cannot make the world into the ideal world they have in mind, so they come to work on themselves. They learn that working on themselves involves working on the world and changing themselves results in changing the world. We are linked inseparably with our circumstances—just starting to study this constructive lifestyle changes our circumstances and so changes us.

Ken lives in his office-warehouse. He rarely leaves it. All around him are reminders of the current sad state of his business. He feels guilty about some of his business practices; he worries about losing money in recent ventures; he despairs when he makes money because of increased income-tax assessments; he avoids bringing his accounting system up to date; he feels trapped and isolated and alienated. Ken is miserable. It is a tragic observation that Ken doesn't seem to be miserable enough! If he were suffering more he might get out of his work setting, find an apartment, try some classes at a local community college, join a club, expand his world beyond buying and selling.

The more Ken complains about his circumstances the angrier

and more hopeless he becomes. There is initially some release when we get something off our chest, a catharsis. But continued complaining simply makes us skillful complainers. One of Ken's assignments, one he frequently forgets, is to refrain from pouring out his troubles in his everyday contacts with others. Not only does it become unpleasant for his friends and relatives to listen to his tirades, but it is unproductive for Ken. He must get his mind off himself and onto what must be done to improve his situation. When Ken becomes a leaning post for others his problems will begin to reduce their dimensions in his mind. Note the order of change that it necessary: It is not that we must somehow straighten out Ken in order to make him worthy of and helpful to others. Instead, Ken must start becoming a listening support to others and then he will begin to straighten out. The constructive doing can and must precede feeling ready to undertake a self-giving project.

Sol was pressured by a friend to sniff cocaine at a party. Frightened, Sol pretended to try it but concealed the drug and threw it away later. Cocaine would have been an easy temporary escape from misery for this affluent middle-aged bachelor. But something in Sol is willing to endure suffering a bit longer in order to embrace a more constructive solution to his misery. Sol is also resisting pressures from his family to return to live with them and to pursue the career they have selected for him. All this resistance is difficult and painful for Sol. But it reflects a solid core of strength and good judgment that isn't giving in to immediate discomfort.

On the other hand, like Ken, Sol isn't hurting enough. His unpleasant work situation, his lying in bed in the mornings, his failure to seek anything more than sexual contacts with women, his inattention to his physical condition and appearance, and his dependency on his family keep him in a state of suffering that prompts complaints and self-criticism but very little action to change his circumstances. If he were more miserable he might become desperate enough to work himself out of these conditions.

"People are always letting me down," complains Frank. He finds us all lacking.

Frank is a fundraiser, middle-aged, with big eyes and a boyish smile. He is a flower child of the sixties grown up into a businessman of the eighties. He is pulled between the innocent search for some sort of spiritual transcendence and the cutthroat world of moneymaking. Now guilty, now gloating; now seeing through the crap, now diving into it. Frank's LSD insights are sometimes blurred by el dinero, but not erased. He longs for something beyond the dollar sign. His life reverberates with disappointment.

When business goes well Frank drifts and drinks and falls behind in his commitments to the world. When his business and personal worlds inevitably collapse Frank hurts and buckles down and catches up on his debts. Then, predictably, life goes pretty well for the next half-cycle.

Sometimes we wonder together, Frank and I, which is better for him—feast or famine? Good times or bad? And we wonder, "Which are the good times?"

A Constructive Living
Approach to Athletics

Athletics involves the training of the body and the mind. So does constructive living. The football lineman who loses the snap count and jumps offside, the tennis pro who slips in concentration and loses a crucial point, the boxer whose guard drops, the runner who forgets her pacing, the baseball pitcher who puts the ball high out of the strike zone, the daydreaming outfielder, the self-conscious bowler, the golfer whose attention lapses during a putt—all have been hindered by inattention or misattention to what reality has brought that needs to be done. The context of this essay is athletics, but the principles are the same throughout constructive living. Remember, the ultimate advantage of this method is to prepare us to live and to die well, with full attention. Whatever our religious beliefs, we would all like to live effectively and to face death well when the time comes.

But here the application of the principles is to sport. What sorts of suggestions can be made from this point of view? First, let us consider the quality of practice. When I am training or coaching or consulting with athletes, one of the first things I look at is the "in-between moment." During a practice session there are likely to be moments when the athlete is standing around waiting for a turn, waiting for the ball, taking a breather, adjusting equipment, being taped, waiting for instructions, and the like. Those times are likely to be lost to practice; worse, they promote inattention that serious athletes cannot afford. Focused attention is a habit that is developed as any skill is developed—by practice and repetition. These in-between moments must not be lost during practice. They can be used to observe other players, to exercise and review athletic movements, to read charts and game plans, to image the upcoming competition, to create strategies and tactics, to listen to the coaching of others, to confer with teammates about the practice, and so on. Each sport and each athlete has particular uses for these in-between moments. But in every case the attention to using these brief periods sharpens the concentration and decreases the likelihood of lapses during the contest.

During a contest there are moments that I call asides. They are the equivalents to the in-between moments of practice. What is the constructive player to do when a member of the other team jumps offside and a penalty is being assessed, what needs doing when a tennis serve is out and we wait for the second serve, what to do in boxing when the opponent has been knocked down and the count is in progress, when a fly ball is hit to the opposite field, while another team member is bowling? Asides like these occur in every sport. These moments may prompt loss of concentration in the participants, a sort of tuning out until play resumes that directly concerns them. Players who aspire to improve their game use these moments constructively, too. They are constantly asking themselves, "Now, what needs to be done?" or simply, "Now, what?" even during these temporary periods of inactivity.

The winning athlete makes every action, on the field and off, purposeful. He or she has determined whether to look at the opponent's eyes or not, and why, what amount of training is necessary so as not to overtrain or undertrain, whether to take risks or aim for consistency, whether to hit for winners or for control, whether to play wide open or with ball control, how to pace the laps. The plans are always built around clear purpose. The constructive competitor is always aware of purpose. Purposes can change in mid-game—for example, when the current strategy isn't working or when the opponent is weaker than we thought. Our purposes can and should be shifted with shifting circumstances. When wind or rain turns up, when we face an unexpected substitute opponent, when an ankle becomes weak or a wrist is sprained, the ability to flexibly revise our goals and means is vital. Reality brings a variety of unexpected circumstances for our response. But, always, there remains the awareness of what the current goal is and why we are playing the way we are in order to achieve it.

Confidence is a necessary element in winning athletics. As we emphasize again and again, confidence *follows* success. The young athlete wants confidence right from the start. Such a desire is seldom realized. One of the purposes of a training session is to provide the occasion for successful accomplishment so that confidence grows. The practice sessions are more than repetitious physical activity. They prepare the athletes psychologically through successful competition with themselves or with others.

Sports activities provide a microcosm of life. The quality with which we play affects the way we live outside the arena. The way we live our everyday lives affects our play, also. All of life deserves our attention . . . even our daydreaming, listening to records, relaxing on the beach. The quality of attention invested enriches our lives and guards against our just existing through moments, missing their contributions to our lives because, though awake, we were mentally asleep.

Morita on Constructive Living

There is little of Morita's original writing translated into English. His collected works fill seven thick volumes in Japanese. Much of what is available in Japan is difficult reading even for younger Japanese therapists because it is written in an older language style rather than revised and simplified modern written characters. Recently an edited collection of Morita's writings on the subject of psychotherapy was published in Japan using the modern characters. *Seishin Ryoho Kogi* presents a clear picture of Morita's views on a number of key issues in his style of personal growth. In this chapter I present a modern interpretation of what he wrote some sixty years ago. The focus here is on the psychotherapeutic aspect of thawing the ice in our lives, although there is much that can be learned about constructive living outside the psychotherapeutic setting. The numbers in parentheses are page numbers from the book *Seishin Ryoho Kogi*.

SHINKEISHITSU CHARACTER

Morita therapy was originally developed for the treatment of people with neurotic characteristics that Morita called *shinkeishitsu*. Shinkeishitsu characteristics include introversion, extreme sensitivity, hypochondriacal tendencies, obsession with details, intelligence, anticipatory anxiety, self-focus (though these people are not as selfish as hysterics), rationality, and constant worrying and rumination (67).

A particular attitude toward illness and bodily functions is characteristic of shinkeishitsu persons. There is a sort of psychological set to perceive trivial and normal physiological responses as unique and harmful, some form of illness (52–53). Such people think that they are ill whether ill or not. Many of us have had shinkeishitsu moments, unnecessarily worrying about some natural physiological process.

In a quiet room the sounds of our heartbeat and breathing and swallowing and pulse may become exaggerated, out of rhythm, perhaps frightening, unharmonious. We may notice a ringing in our ears. In contrast, steady stimuli, even when strong, may go unnoticed after we have adapted to them in our ordinary environment.

Morita was well aware that the subjective recognition or discovery of a disease is part of the disease itself, part of the experience of it, part of the psychological aspect of any disease (or nondisease, as in the case of the shinkeishitsu person's misperception of a normal physiological response like ringing in the ears). One can have a disease and not be aware of it, Morita pointed out; then the psychological aspect of suffering from knowledge that one is ill would be lacking. Discovery of illness as the result of a phsyician's examination would add this psychological dimension. Even if a misdiagnosis was involved and the patient was incorrectly told that he or she was ill, the psychological aspect would be present without the illness. The psychological facet doesn't govern the physical facet (we can think ourselves to be well and be quite ill), but there is a subjective aspect of discomfort when one considers oneself to be ill (48–49).

It can be said that everyone has some shinkeishitsu characteristics (49). The stronger the shinkeishitsu, the stronger the psychological, subjective component of an illness. Morita noted that we can treat this component in anyone (49).

The sudden cessation of background noise or other stimulus,

or a change in the level of some stimulus, attracts our attention. The sensitive shinkeishitsu may try to escape from upsetting stimuli, but escape isn't possible due to these perceptual characteristics. When someone runs away to the country to escape the loud sounds of city traffic, he may be bothered by the sounds of the water dripping from the farmhouse roof. So there is always a tradeoff when certain stimuli are reduced, because the sensitivity lies in the sensory perception of the person and not simply in the intensity of the stimuli.

It is possible, however, to selectively reduce certain inputs for particular purposes (109). In some problems of love it may be more effective to effect a complete cutoff of contact and reminders of the loved one in order to allow other stimuli to emerge from background. Clients may need isolation from family influence in order to develop new living patterns (111). Opportunities to complain to friends or family increase attention to and effects of symptoms. Family sympathy and encouragement of dependency may increase symptoms (112). Thus, for some clients the isolation of absolute bedrest and inpatient training become necessary. These methods both remove the client from stimuli that may contribute to the disorder and demonstrate to the client through experience that escape from all discomforting stimuli is impossible.

Not only do shinkeishitsu react with oversensitivity to stimuli, they actually create or generate unpleasant stimuli through anticipation and imagination even when no external source exists in reality. As one worries about how one's spouse will react to news about moving or frets about how many problems might have been answered incorrectly on an examination or envisions difficult questions being put forth during an interview, anticipatory anxiety is being generated. This anticipation of trouble can produce further difficulties as a self-fulfilling prophecy (52). The worry about an upcoming interview can foster insomnia, for example, resulting in tiredness and a poor interview.

Morita contrasted shinkeishitsu and hysteric personality types. Although shinkeishitsu persons are extremely conscious of feared and unpleasant situations and very aware of their fears, hysteric persons are not. Hysteric individuals, unaware of their fear, translate it into hysterical paralysis and other bodily symptoms (49–50). Freudian theory, with its emphasis on the unconscious, seems to be based on this characteristic lack of awareness of hysterics.

Morita saw hysteria as a basic lack of harmony between feelings and knowledge of those feelings (53). He considered hysteria to be a reflection of childlike immaturity and self-centeredness. Hysteric people are readily pushed about by their own shifting emotions, but they are relatively insensitive to the feelings of others. When they have no immediate troubles they tend to be asymptomatic, unlike the shinkeishitsu people, who anticipate problems even when there are none. In addition, Morita described hysterics as lacking reservation, thoughtless of others, complaining, feeling unloved and that they lack sympathy from others, extremely changeable in mood and action, capable of moments of compassion and love and self-sacrifice (but because these moments are emotionally induced they aren't lasting). Hysterics are less rational and intellectual than shinkeishitsu types so they are less subject to influence by explanations (68).

Just as everyone has some shinkeishitsu characteristics and moments, so everyone has some hysteric characteristics and moments, too (50).

Morita therapy is effective with the shinkeishitsu but also with the hysteric elements of our characters (139). Isolation, education, and guided living produce a stronger will, courage, confidence, and decisiveness (118). Physical activity, especially work, helps shinkeishitsu people get out of their mental wheelspinning, helps hysterics to free themselves from being pushed about by their feelings, and helps all of us feel a sense of responsibility and self-worth. Even psychotics benefit from physical activity, which results in a reduction in delusions (133).

Morita was well aware of the limitations of some of the other techniques for curing neurosis prevalent in his time, techniques still used by some therapists today. Mere admonition and attempts at intellectual persuasion were seen by Morita to be insufficient in treating the neurotic sides of ourselves. To say, "Live in the pres-

DAVID K. REYNOLDS

ent," "Forget the past," "There is no need to dwell on suffering," "Be confident," and the like has no lasting effect on us. Persuasion must be experience-based. That is, the Moritist guide must explain, then guide the patient to have an experience. As a result of the experience there is belief and real understanding (137). Morita pointed out that no one cures patients with theory (138). Theoretically, it is natural to die, but when we face death there is not necessarily an emotional acceptance of that theory (138).

Similarly, the disadvantage of suggestion is that it reduces the patients' ability to judge for themselves (182). It is a superficial solution to the problems posed by neurosis. Perceptively, Morita saw that the disadvantage of creating feelings of peacefulness through breathing exercises is that the exercises are, in the main, only useful when we are doing them. They are not adaptable to the conditions of everyday life (166). Sometimes we need excitement, not peacefulness, in order to get something done. When I am fleeing a fire or running a football pass pattern I don't want to be perfectly calm. Breathing exercises are an inflexible method of responding to the variety of situations that reality provides us (167). Morita sought a technique that would change the fundamental responses of his clients to everyday circumstances. It was not enough to work on the symptoms of the moment. Today, assertiveness training and some forms of behavior therapy are subject to the same criticisms. They are inflexible and unresponsive to the changing reality to which everyone must adapt and respond.

From the above we can see that Morita considered all neuroses as problems of character—lack of maturity, improper understanding, disharmony. Therefore, rest and character development training followed as natural elements of cure. Perhaps the rest aspect came from the medical side of his training. There has been a historical change in Morita therapy in Japan and in the United States de-emphasizing rest as part of his twofold attack on neurosis.

BEDREST IN MORITA THERAPY

There was a time when many Westerners equated Morita therapy with isolated bedrest. They were unaware of the uses of Morita's ideas in outpatient clinics, group meetings, and correspondence therapy. In Japan today there are only a dozen or so hospitals and clinics where isolated bedrest is offered at all. It is likely that in twenty years there will be only a few such hospitals. In the future, bedrest may be offered in nonmedical retreat settings. What is this unusual treatment mode? How does it work? What is its purpose? When is it used in Japan and in the United States? How does it fit into Moritist theory?

Morita's *shinshin doitsu* theory holds that body and mind are two aspects of the same thing. The psyche is our life activity (23). Whatever is happening to our bodies not only affects our bodies, it is happening to our psyches, as well. It takes some effort to understand body and psyche as the same thing, in contrast to the more common Western interpretation that they are intimately connected but separate. From Morita's perspective there is only a single embodied mind or activated body, depending upon which aspect of the whole we wish to emphasize at the time. Absolute bedrest, then, will produce some profound effect on this bodymind because it is a profound change in life activity.

The isolated bedrest technique involved lying in bed, usually for a week in a private room. The clients aren't allowed to read or write or talk or watch television or listen to the radio or engage in any distracting activities. Meals are served three times a day to the bedside of the clients. They are allowed to brush their teeth, go to the bathroom, wash their faces in the morning, and bathe once during the week. Rules vary slightly from one hospital to another. In some Moritist hospitals in Japan, the therapist visits the client daily for a brief check on progress. In others, the patient is called from his room daily to appear briefly before the therapist. The essence of bedrest is the long period of idle rest with no escape from the productions of the client's own mind.

Morita believed that isolated bedrest is necessary for some patients. Travel, vacations, or simply staying at home would not provide sufficient diminishing or change of stimuli. Taking time off from work for social visiting and play could be exhausting for some patients (99). Socializing with an extrovert tends to tire a shinkeishitsu person; socializing with another shinkeishitsu person is likely to lead to complaining, which directs attention to symptoms, thereby magnifying them (147). In general, Morita preferred sending patients to work or to school rather than to travel or even to bed. Part of the low self-esteem of our patients comes from failure to live up their own standards; they are tense, in part, because of their awareness of their own irresponsibility. Morita refused to allow them to flee from their debt to the world in numerous job changes and vacations (147). Even in periods of unemployment, clients can work around the house and seek work through applications, interviews, and searching through classified ads. But when the patients' neuroses were so severe that they weren't going to work or school, the need, Morita felt, was for the constant low stimuli surroundings of isolated absolute bedrest.

When we have a natural input of stimuli our thoughts flow in natural pace from input to input. Even when we stop moving about and sit quietly our thoughts continue to flow, we ruminate. Our minds generate the stimulus input that our movement no longer stimulates. As we walk in a field we see a flower, then we want to go over and pick it, then we must find a vase to put it in, then we need to arrange it and put it on a stand—all the natural consequences of seeing the flower. In a pitch-dark room our minds create movement and lights through imagination; in the quiet of night sounds are exaggerated and interpreted on the basis of little information (107). As noted above, in a soundless room the sounds of heartbeat and breathing and swallowing and pulse become exaggerated. Morita recommended that a night-light be provided so that the person undergoing bedrest wouldn't have the imagination stimulated by pitch-darkness (94). He also recommended a vase with fresh flowers be placed in the patient's room during bedrest.

So bedrest interrupts the organization of attention that activity provides. Organs continue to function (e.g., the heart continues beating) and the mind continues to churn out ideas and associations and feelings and the like. Bedrest acts initially to disrupt old habit patterns. It begins to create disharmony within the bodymind

(124). Attention turns inward to the mind-generated stimuli. But as the week progresses toward its end, the bodymind begins once more to find harmony, on a quieter level. There comes an increasing acceptance of mental productions along with a clear understanding of the necessity of bodily activity to keep the mind satisfactorily stocked with reality-based input.

Morita noticed that much (a) psychological and (b) physical pain—more properly, experienced pain that seems to have (a) some locus or (b) no locus in the body—passes as we wait and rest. His perspective was anti-Freudian in that Morita held that the more we express feelings (that is, the more we talk about them, complain about them) the more we stimulate them, and the stronger they become (97). He was so convinced of the value of bedrest that sometimes Morita pressured some patients to begin bedrest, a practice we would not condone today (113).

He listed three purposes of bedrest in his writings. The first is diagnostic. Bedrest is a kind of constant circumstance (somewhat like the ambiguous blots of ink in a Rorschach test) within which the client's character will find expression in some behavioral response. Certain psychotic patients find no boredom during bedrest, even when it extends longer than a week. Shinkeishitsu persons find it uncomfortable, but they are able to endure it. Hysterics and some sociopaths will leave bedrest when it becomes uncomfortable for them.

The danger of bedrest is primarily for depressed patients. There is some risk of suicide with clinically depressed individuals, so careful diagnosis and close monitoring coupled with the careful use of antidepressant drugs are necessary for such cases.

The second purpose of isolated bedrest is to bring the mind and body into harmony through rest. Morita used Zen phrases to describe the simplification of desires that occurs during this retreat from the ordinary world (102). The third purpose is to face the self. There is no escape from one's own thoughts and feelings during bedrest—no radio, no books, no television, no distracting conversations. What drift to the surface of awareness during these days of constant low stimuli are the constructions of the mind. There is no recourse but to face them.

DAVID K. REYNOLDS

Morita found that shinkeishitsu clients usually run a rather predictable course during bedrest. The first day is not particularly unpleasant for them. From the second day they begin to suffer. They are unable to sleep; they complain of pains. For some the peak discomfort is reached during the second day, for others somewhat later. After two or three hours of intense suffering it takes only ten or twenty minutes to give in to the mental anguish or, perhaps, to go through it. When we merge with suffering it disappears; Morita described the attitude as that of someone with only five more minutes of life left on a battlefield. Necessary death brings necessary victory (102). Then follows the relief of acceptance (103). During day three some patients are amazed at this newfound relief. They try to create their previous state experimentally but find that they cannot. They discover experientially their lack of control over their feelings. The fourth day they are bored and begin looking at the specific details of their past life with feelings of despair (104). In the final phase of bedrest the patient wants to be active and engaged in life. This desire to participate in the world outside the bedroom motivates the patient to seek contact with the real world.

RELIGION AND DEATH

Neurosis is an educational problem, not a medical problem. Neurotic symptoms are always the result of misguided thinking and behavior (138). Morita held that the most important factors in relieving neuroses are the proper views of human living, effort, and patience (71). He believed that genuine religion could be helpful in treating neuroses—read ignorance (71). But he also saw that much of what went under the guise of religion was no more than elaborate self-seeking. Formal religious institutions in Morita's day, and in our own, had become little more than edifices built on word games. Morita had no patience with games of words because they offered no value to daily living (26).

In Morita's view the basic fear of all humans is death. Fear of illness is rooted in this fear of death. Morita believed that no one can avoid the fear and sorrow associated with dying. Although some people may say that they can handle it coolly, when faced with the experience of terminality they, too, feel some anxiety. Again, theory and reality are different. Even elderly patients who say that they wish to die soon resist when faced with the immediacy of their own death. Their feelings don't correspond with their thinking about death (62–63).

In Morita's experience, when patients were told that they had a terminal disease they were shocked and filled with despair. Then these feelings faded and they wanted to live the next year or the next week or the next day. They always held hope that cure was possible. Those who eventually succumbed to chronic illness gradually weakened until the desire to fight death faded, consciousness drifted, and they expired peacefully, like a dying fire (66–67).

Morita noticed that some patients can stave off death until they see a beloved child, and then die. He also observed that the completion of a task or a change in physical conditions for the better could create sudden relief and result in untimely death (63). We know that job promotions can be stressful and are related to some suicides.

In general, Morita was an acute observer of the human condition. Not only do we fear death, he noted, but we fear the living death of failure, of not achieving our potential. We fear social and psychological death, too. This drive to live also prompts us to want to live fully. Those with a strong lust for life *(sei no yokubo)* are pushed to try to achieve greatness. Those who are driven to achieve, to develop their potential, must reach some balance between their desires and their fears. Behind every distressing fear is a strong positive desire.

We cannot retreat from the world to protect ourselves from harm and still achieve the best of which we are capable. We cannot grow without risking our social/psychological/physical lives. The tension between our fear of dying and our drive to live fully is transcended when we become purpose focused in our living. The issue of the paralyzing fear of failure drops from our minds as our attention turns toward doing what needs to be done in this moment.

DAVID K. REYNOLDS

Psychological Buddhism and Constructive Living

The constructive lifestyle described in this book is not Buddhist in a religious sense. I am not a Buddhist, although some of my students are. Nevertheless, there is a useful psychology of human life that has been developed by people who called themselves (or were called by their contemporaries) Buddhists. In particular, the insights of those who followed the path of Zen shed light on the everyday functioning of the human mind. Zen, too, has a religious aspect and a psychological aspect. We can work on melting the glaciers of our lives without concerning ourselves at all with Buddhist beliefs or the institutional Buddhist church. But I think we cannot effectively bring warmth into our lives if we ignore the psychological principles of Zen. In this chapter I have drawn together some quotes from Buddhist psychology literature to illustrate how they parallel and inform the psychological principles of constructive living.

In more than one sense, work is an effective icebreaker.

CONSTRUCTIVE ACTIVITY

One of the basic notions of our system is that constructive activity is possible despite ups and downs in feelings. It is the presence of constructive activity in a student's life that tells me how the student is progressing in understanding this lifeway. More than the length of their study, more than their ability to give proper answers to questions about theory and practice, more than the number of books and articles read on the subject, more than the number of workshops attended, even more than the reduction of their troubling symptoms or increased confidence and satisfaction with life, the amount of constructive activity in students' everyday lives tells me the level of their advancement in this lifeway. For centuries Zen masters have extolled the value of doing what needs doing as an important element in spiritual/psychological development.

"A contemporary Zen master has said that 'Zen is picking up your coat from the floor and hanging it up.' That is all that is required, and nothing could be simpler. Yet how difficult! There is no fun in 'picking up your coat,' and all such tasks are not at all self-fulling and enriching. They do not make us richer, or more powerful, or sexier, or more personable. How much more rewarding and fun it is just to read another book on self-improvement, or spend the day at the beach, watch television, go to a party, take a course in self-assertiveness, or join a protest demonstration for the latest cause. Worse, however, is the fact that 'picking up your coat' doesn't seem to be a very 'spiritual' kind of practice, like prayer, meditation, fasting, or developing a meaningful relationship. There is nothing more ordinary and unspecial than 'picking up your coat.' Yet, it is really the essence of practice, for 'picking up your coat' is exactly what Dogen means by meditation" (Cook, 1978, p. 11).

"In Buddhism the fruits of work, getting things done, are not separate from doing things. There is no great plan or goal yet everything in its own time gets accomplished. . . .

"Work when done with the correct attitude can help us overcome our ego-centeredness and, if wholeheartedly engaged in, can enliven and energize the body-mind; its benefits therefore can never be emphasized enough. Zen master Daie says, 'Zazen in motion is a million times greater in value than zazen in quietude.' . . .

"The person who is able in no matter *what* circumstances to

DAVID K. REYNOLDS

devote himself or herself totally to the task at hand has reached a . . . profound level.

"Work is not something you do with just your hands—it is done with your entire being. This is no mere power of positive thinking. In doing any task, we must *just* do it.

"As Master Han Shan has said, 'When the Work goes well, things in the outer world won't bother you very much.' When the Work goes well, then work goes well.

"A vocation gives a framework within which to consolidate and focus the life force in its many and varied aspects. It begins to work on us and inspires and supports us" ("Work," *Zen Bow*, 1977, pp. 59–64).

The emphasis in our constructive lifestyle is on the quality of the doing and not on the expected results. Results will come from our work, though not always the results we want or expect. These results, whatever they might be, indicate to us what needs to be done next.

"Still, there should be no regret even if a thing conceived and begun is not completed: if even one pillar is set up, I do not care if [i.e., as long as] in the future they shall see that someone had conceived of such an undertaking but could not complete it" (Dogen, trans. Cleary, 1980, p. 34).

Sometimes we fail at a task. To fail means that the work or the result hasn't turned out as we or someone else wanted or expected. That circumstance, too, is interesting and presents other tasks for our attention and action.

"When we do wrong or make mistakes, we go on with renewed vigour to the next task; a faux pas cannot check us or make us dwell on it with self-torturing shame" (Blyth, 1948, pp. 206–207).

True failure, however, comes from not doing what we know needs doing. When we don't put forth the effort reality has no accurate way of informing us of what would have resulted from that action. Too many of my students, coming from Western psychotherapies, are overly skillful at asking questions and probing for insights as escapes from taking direct necessary action in their lives. They have become lazy about their everyday life work.

"People ask why and how as an excuse for not doing what they know they should do" (Blyth, 1948, p. 228).

"And if the enlightenment is real, it must be, as Ungan and Blake said, 'in minute details' of daily life" (Blyth, 1948, p. 237).

> A sentence which does not reveal its meaning
> Attains its end before being spoken.
> You press forward, with mouth a-chatter
> Betraying your not knowing what to do.
> —UMMON (Blyth, 1978, p. 255)

Why is it that students begin by expecting the transmission of mystical, esoteric knowledge? I keep saying and writing the simplest of messages. They are not complicated or difficult to understand. They can be readily verified through daily behavior. The difficulty lies "only" in the moment-by-moment practice.

"Nansen said, 'Up to today, you and I, Brother, have talked over things, and I know how you think, but afterwards, if someone should ask me about your opinion of the most important thing in the world, what should I say?' Kisu said, 'This piece of land here would be a nice place to build a hermitage on.' Nansen said, 'Never mind about building any hermitages, what is your opinion of the most important thing in the world?' Kisu gulped down his tea and stood up. Nansen said, 'Brother, you have drunk your tea, but I haven't finished mine yet!' Kisu said, 'If you talk as you have been, not a drop of water can be finished up.' Nansen was silent, and went off.

"'The most important thing in the world' is always what a man is doing at this moment" (Blyth, 1948, pp. 263–264).

One of the gratifying by-products of the warmth generated by purposeful activity is a recognition of how we "fit" in the world. The task at hand concerns one's fellow worker, fellow spouse, fellow lawnmower, fellow telephone, fellow towel, and so forth. Anomie vanishes.

"'Did I switch the light off? I haven't time to go back now and in any case someone else is bound to look after it!' But no, even though there is little time, the journey to check the light switch must be made. A small point, to be sure, but it is precisely in the small points that a staff training program is made. 'Don't waste' is one of the most important lessons to be learned. The sense of personal responsibility for all that happens—not leaving it to others to carry the burden of maintaining the Center—is another. And above all mindfulness, doing things in an alert, aware mindstate, will ensure that light switches are turned off and that what should be done, gets done.

"The state of mind wherein everything is respected as important and unique in its own right, ends with everything becoming an extension of oneself. While to waste is to separate oneself— really to break oneself off—from the rest of the world, to care for things makes the whole world come to life" ("The Staff Program," *Zen Bow*, 1977, pp. 65– 67).

The details of everyday behavior were spelled out in detail for the Zen monks. Every action carried constructive possibility. Every doing was a step toward or away from enlightenment. Suzuki (1965, p. 153) cites the Regulations of the Official Quarters of the Zen monastery: "10. The sandals are not to be left carelessly on the floor. While stepping up and down the hall, do not make rustling sounds. Do not make light of the trivial deeds of daily life, for great virtues are born of them. . . ."

REALITY, RIGHT NOW

We live in this moment only. Now this moment. Now this. Our minds create images in the present of moments past and moments future. Our minds generate recollections of past selves and images of future selves. But if our lives are to melt into reality, they must do so in this now or this now or this now. For now is all we have with which to work.

"I'm perfectly willing to wash dishes too, because the art of washing dishes is that you only have to wash one at a time. If you're doing it day after day you have in your mind's eye an enormous stack of filthy dishes which you have washed in years past and an enormous stack of filthy dishes which you will wash in future years. But if you bring your mind to the state of reality which is only now, this is where we are, you only have to wash one dish. It's the only dish you'll ever have to wash. You ignore all the rest, because in reality there is no past and there is no future. There is just now. So you wash this one" (Watts, 1974, p. 137).

"But actually one cannot go back literally. One does not really have to go back. Rather one discovers what one was by the process of going more deeply into the present situation. That is the difference between an intuitive approach and an intellectual one. You can go back intellectually, but that does not help; you remain stuck in the same point of view. The whole idea is that if you are able to realize what you are at the present moment, you do not need to try to go back. What you are at this moment contains the whole message of what you were" (Trungpa, 1975, p. 14).

"If a person is able to meet the present situation . . . the present coincidence, as it is, a person can develop tremendous confidence. He begins to see that no one is organizing the situation for him but that he can work for himself. He develops a tremendous feeling of spaciousness because the future is a completely open one" (Trungpa, 1975, p. 79).

Many of our exercises encourage the student to make contact with the experiences of this present moment. In the deepest sense, the student is not *my* student but the student of reality. I am merely one aspect of the student's present reality that asks for some of the student's attention. But so do the stairs and the phonograph record and the rival at the office and the door that sticks and the frosted glass and so on.

"The wisdom of dealing with situations as they are, and that is what wisdom is, contains tremendous precision that could not come from anywhere else but the physical situations of sight, smell, feeling, touchable objects, and sounds. The earthy situation of actual things as they are is the source of wisdom" (Trungpa, 1975. p. 10).

Seeking the Magical Brazier

How desperately and persistently my students seek salvation outside of themselves! They are certain that there is some wonderful warming current that will melt the ice in their lives for them. Sometimes they try to put me in the role of savior. Such effort always leads to disappointment. I never saved anyone. Until the students learn to melt into reality they remain frozen hard in their self-consciousness:

If I changed my therapist perhaps I'd get better.

If I moved closer to (farther from) my work (my lover, that nicer section of town, a religious facility, the hospital) life would go well for me.

If I took the right combination of medications (vitamins, herbs) all the trouble with my emotions would go away.

If my family (the bank, my boss) gave me the money I need to start over I wouldn't have any more problems.

If I changed jobs (lovers, dreams) all would be fine.

If I could just find a good man (woman) I could settle down and my worries would be over.

If I felt better (had more confidence, worried less, felt braver, loved myself more) I'd make some solid changes in my life.

The search for sources of salvation never ceases. When I challenge the search itself my student may become quite emotional.

There is some comfort in believing that there exists somewhere a saving condition, whether it is in our grasp or not. Unfortunately (or fortunately), there is no salvation from outside. There is only acceptance and proper action. There is only holding to purpose through storms of emotion. There is only understanding and acting based on best knowledge. The soft padding is gone, but the resources are sufficient and dependable, in time.

Warming Trend

Today I crossed the street without waiting because a man had already pushed the traffic button for pedestrians. He had waited for the cycle to turn the light red and stop the cars. I walked up just as they stopped. I was grateful that his waiting had expedited my crossing.

Perhaps some Westerners would wonder at my sense of gratitude. He pushed the button so that he could cross the street and not for my convenience. Of course, I did benefit from his action. But my benefit was not his intent. Still, his action served me, whatever his intent. Where should we draw the line of gratitude? People buy my books not to support me, but the result is that I am supported. Do they deserve my gratitude? Yes, I believe that they do. But then salespeople sell shoes to people like me in order to make their living; do they merit my gratitude for my shoes even though I paid for them? Yes, they do.

Democratic capitalism has become a sort of self-centered enterprise. The theory is that some balance can be achieved as all of us act in our own self-interest. When I exceed my bounds your self-interest will push me back into line. No one can expect that you will sacrifice your success for my interest. A chilling wind drifts through the crevices of this socioeconomic system. I owe you something even though I have paid a fair price for your service. You owe me something for asking you to serve me. We are favoring each other with our business on a dimension other than the one of economic transaction.

We all sense this difference between balanced self-interest and the dimensions of human favor. That is why we prefer to shop at stores where the employees and management seem actually grateful for our patronage. It is why we feel offended by postal employees who act as though they do us a favor by selling stamps. Mutual gratitude glides along above an exchange of equal value, making the transactions and us glow.

But whether or not those who do me favors (knowingly or not, intentionally or not) reciprocate my gratitude, my feelings and words of thanks are due them.

I'm grateful to my toothpaste for cleaning my teeth and to the manufacturer for making the toothpaste. In our society the consumer is often seen to be aligned against the producer (as labor is aligned against management). It is refreshing to consider the service I receive and the debt I owe to those whose products ease and enrich my life.

This attitude is part of the treasuring of all things because all things are borrowed. There is nothing that is truly mine. What I bought was paid for with money received from others. The money was earned with my time and effort; but these outputs, too, are possible only because of the training I received from others, the food for energy, the body that was a gift from my parents, and so forth. As I trace back everything that appears to be "mine" it evaporates into the plethora of debts I owe the world.

Taking it a step further I am but a reflection of these efforts of others. I am the product of my surroundings, surroundings that extend back in time to eras even before my birth. How much I owe to Edison and Lincoln and Columbus and Plato and some unnamed protohominid ancestor, to those who sowed and sewed to keep my ancestors alive, to the corn and cotton, the sun, the melting snow. Back and back, the closer I look the wider the net of interconnections—it is not a widening tunnel of gratitude, but an embracing totality that exists now and extends into past and future equally encompassing.

It seems appropriate to say that I *am* my surroundings. What is there that is mine that is separate from them? I become you, too. Thank you for your contribution to this part of this moment/circumstance that I call "me."

Facts, Truth, and Ideas

Some of the unnecessary trouble and suffering we humans endure comes from our failure to distinguish among facts, truth, and reality. Ideas, for example, are real. They may be right or wrong when compared with facts or with truth, but they are real in the sense that they exist in our minds. They come from the unknown and are understandable to us as we think them. They help form our opinions and beliefs and prejudices and preferences. They are as natural as wind and ocean spray. They influence what we do just like the weather, an illness, a marriage, or a new car—and you will find few who would deny the reality of these.

On another level are facts. Facts are interpreted aspects of reality. Many people these days use the scientific method to discover and verify facts. But what is considered a fact today may be disputed and disproved tomorrow. Science allows for the overturning of facts—even more, it is built on the very premise that facts can be deposed but never fully proved. We can find evidence to support a view of a fact, but there always remains the possibility of a future discovery that will provide a contrary case which will force us to modify our view of that fact. The scientific method and the legal system and logical investigation and other techniques provide means by which people define facts. All these techniques involve reflection on (interpreting) some action. For example, the chemist does something with chemicals and observes the results and reflects upon his or her findings and presents the facts for others' consideration and verification.

On still another level is truth. We verify truth by reflecting on some actions, too. We may hear about a truth or read about it, but it is never truth for us unless it is grounded in our own experience, our behavior. Truth never changes. It is unlike reality and unlike facts in this regard. We have a sense of confidence and commitment to truth that is not extended to reality and to facts. Others may argue us out of our prejudices and beliefs, reality keeps on changing before our eyes, and facts can be shown to be false. But truth remains firm despite all these other changes and potential changes. When we have encountered truth experientially, we "know" its validity even though we may try to hide from it or ignore it or act in opposition to it.

Reality keeps presenting us with something needing to be done. Verify the truth of this statement for yourself.

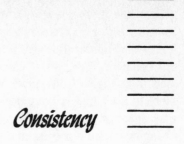

Consistency

Whenever one reads a list of traditional Japanese character traits the list includes qualities like patience, endurance, or tenacity. The Japanese have found something important here. Steady persistence even in the face of great difficulties can often produce favorable results.

There is likely to be an important difference between the way a mature adult and a young teenager water a garden. That daily job isn't particularly difficult—it doesn't take long experience or great strength to do the task. The difference between adult and youth may not appear for a couple of weeks. But, in time, the youth may water unevenly, hurriedly. The mature adult waters carefully each time, whether it is the first or the fiftieth.

The psychiatrist Tomio Hirai found that the experienced Zen Buddhist meditator's brain waves responded to a clicking sound exactly the same on the fiftieth as on the first click. Inexperienced meditators' brains responded to the first clicks, but they seemed to filter out or ignore the later clicking sounds. It was as though the inexperienced meditators' minds were saying, "Oh, that's just another of those bothersome clicks; it's not worth my attention anymore." The steady consistency of response hadn't yet been developed in the beginners.

The principle of consistency applies to words of politeness and words of appreciation for someone's kindness, effort, and service. It is easy to use words of gratitude during courtship days, during the first days of a visit with relatives, or an initial period on a new job. Then with time and familiarity and repetition comes a taking for granted, an ignoring of others' acts of kindness. Certainly, words of appreciation are likely to decline over time unless we make a special effort to notice others' efforts and acknowledge them.

Some will say that closeness in a relationship obviates the necessity for such words. "Love is never having to say you're sorry." Such an attitude is mistaken. Consistency in polite expressions of gratitude and apology is necessary both for those who receive them and for those who offer them. We all like to be told we are appreciated. It isn't difficult to recognize the value of hearing a word of thanks. But there is equal value to the one who says, "Thank you." The steady effort to put out these small words affects the speaker, too. The words symbolize alert recognition of others' services and others' value in our lives. The words mean that our convenience is less important than our companion's ears. By ignoring others' contributions or failing to make an overt response to them, we belittle their efforts and fail to remind ourselves of the everyday services that surround and support us.

The person who fails to note and acknowledge surrounding kindness becomes "dry" and isolated. Persistent tributes to others' efforts in our behalf leads to an appreciation of their worth and of our own worth to them. The warmth of these simple words gently melts summer ice.

Situational Context and Psychiatric Diagnosis

In April, 1982, psychiatric specialists from forty countries gathered in Copenhagen to consider problems of psychiatric classification. Much attention was paid to cultural differences in symptoms and diagnostic styles. Clearly, the latest manual for standardized diagnoses, *ICD-9*, still emphasizes Western psychiatric syndromes and Western perspectives on diagnosis. Such a Western bias is increasingly seen to be inadequate by the rest of the world. More and more strongly comes the call for more culture-free diagnostic criteria, more non-Western research approaches, and more cross-cultural cooperative studies.

There is, however, a more fundamental difficulty with current psychiatric diagnosis, a difficulty that lies even deeper than cultural differences. That difficulty is the serious lack of attention to the situational context in which psychotic and psychoneurotic symptoms are expressed. To put my criticism in its most extreme form: Behavior (for example, hallucinatory speech, complaints of headaches and stomach pains, hysterical paralysis, insomnia, compulsive eye blinking) has no meaning at all unless one considers the circumstances (the cultural context, the family setting, the immediate social situation) in which the behavior appears. As Magnusson (1981, p. 10) put it, "Behavior takes place in situations; it does not exist except in relation to certain situational conditions and cannot be understood and explained in isolation from them."

In the field of mental disorder R. D. Laing has presented the case for the meaningfulness of schizophrenic behavior within the family context of certain patients. My work with Norman Farberow (1976, 1977, 1981) demonstrates the pragmatic usefulness of the apparently "crazy" behavior of patients on psychiatric wards and in other settings. Similarly, what appears to be insane panic behavior in crowds during building fires makes some sense in terms of the situational context of limited access to fire escape routes.

The point here is that we cannot divorce a behavior from its setting and then try to compare it to a similar behavior in a different setting. But that separation of behavior and setting is precisely what current diagnostic categories try to do. According to current diagnostic methods a hallucination is a hallucination despite the occasion on which it occurs. Compulsive handwashing may be quite useful for the busy surgeon, but it may be a problem behavior for the person who must compulsively wash before fleeing from a burning building. A medical diagnostic system that ignores the context of behavior may work reasonably well in evaluating physical illness (though even physical illness may involve situational considerations, which are currently recognized within, for example, psychosomatic medicine), but it doesn't make sense in functional psychiatric disorders.

Cultural differences are one sort of contextual variable that must be taken into consideration. There may be no patients in the United States who believe that they are the emperor of Japan, but there are such patients in Japan. Involutional melancholia may be rare in Third World countries in which the life expectancy is less than forty years of age. Shyness may stimulate different social responses from significant others in Japan than in America.

But cultural variables are not the only situational considerations that must be taken into account for an adequate system of diagnosis. Within a single country different families have their own family customs and understandings about behavior, and each social class, region, and neighborhood interprets some behaviors differently. Furthermore, each individual acts within an unique set of contexts—stages upon which we act out our roles of life.

A few years ago on a psychiatric ward a long-term patient picked up a discarded yellow tag from the floor and gave it to me as a present. The yellow piece of paper was worth nothing in terms of money; it was trash. Was his giving it to me a sign of his psychosis? He had nothing else to give, no possession to offer me as a token of his friendship. Would he be more "normal" if he had ignored me, knowing that he owned nothing to offer as a symbol of his friendly feelings? His gift-giving behavior can be interpreted as a sign of his insanity or as a sign of his human warmth. Was his action crazier than dropping bombs from an airplane on civilians? The interpretation lies within the context and within the values of the person who is interpreting.

Recently, there has been developing in the West a psychology of situations. Scientists such as David Magnusson in Sweden and Roger Barker, Jack and Jeanne Block, Nancy Cantor, Daryl Bem, Walter Mischel, Norman Endler, and others in the United States and Canada are building theories that consider both circumstances and personality in explaining behavior. It is time for psychiatrists to discard their outmoded notions about the permanence of personality. We all have multiple personalities. We all change our behavior as our situations change. So do our patients. We cannot build descriptions of psychiatric syndromes that are static, unchanging pigeonholes. Our patients are sometimes this, sometimes that; sometimes rational, sometimes irrational; sometimes lucid, sometimes not. But the diagnostic label (such as "schizophrenia" or "psychotic depression") is an unchanging term that ignores the changeability of the patient.

Mental disorders are not like uniform coins, always and invariably occurring in the social transactions of our patients. It is time to develop realistic multidimensional diagnostic categories, categories that consider situational context when interpreting and labeling behavior. Situations change, personalities change. When will our diagnostic categories change in recognition of the moment-by-moment changeableness of all humans?

DAVID K. REYNOLDS

The Future of Morita Therapy as a Constructive Lifestyle *

Let us consider expanding, broadening, outgrowing old definitions and old limits. There are two levels worthy of our thinking here—on the personal level I shall refer to the ways in which we each learn to overcome the limits we place on ourselves. Morita therapy has helped many of us recognize and change the unrealistic limits that clutter our lives. On another level we can reflect upon the ways we can overcome the limits that have been placed on Morita's ideas as a system. I intend to suggest ways in which we can make Morita "therapy" more accessible and helpful to many more people than just those labeled shinkeishitsu neurotic.

OUTGROWING OUR OLD SELVES

The way we discover ourselves, the way we create our identity, is to look back on our past and see what kind of people we were. If we did timid things we see ourselves as timid; if we did adventurous things we see ourselves as adventurous. The way to change the way we see ourselves is to change our past. Right now we are

*In slightly revised form this essay was presented on November 3, 1984, in Tokyo as a lecture in Japanese to a meeting of Seikatsu no Hakkenkai (The Discovery of Life Organization), the largest Moritist establishment in the world.

in the process of creating a new past. What we do now will become our past when we look back on our actions tomorrow. We change who we are by changing what we do. It is easy to see the limits people place on their own lives seeking a return to childhood, security, and certainty. Reality doesn't allow us the safety, security, and certainty of true childhood after we have become adults. We must risk in order to accomplish, in order to succeed, in order to grow.

OUTGROWING THE "THERAPY" LABEL

Therapies, too, have a kind of identity created through their past histories.

There is a history of Morita therapy just as there is a history for each one of us. Morita therapy began as a treatment form for shinkeishitsu neurosis. It was used by physicians to treat this narrow range of neurotic problems in Japan. But over the years it has grown to be used on a wider range of human problems in a number of countries. And it is practiced not only by physicians but by psychologists, social workers, teachers, ministers, businessmen, and others. At one time Morita therapy was practiced only in the home of Morita. Now it is taught in outpatient clinics and in correspondence and in study groups and in retreat settings and in American colleges and in lectures like this. You can see that Morita therapy has grown and broadened. I think that Morita therapy is in a stage of adolescence. Just like an adolescent it is in search of its adult identity.

Some people would like to see Morita therapy remain the narrow domain of elite physicians. They would like to see it return to its childhood like the girl in "The Doll Carriage" (see p. 115). But the hospitals for Morita therapy are few. And the number of young physicians who are truly doing only Morita therapy is small. There is no future for Morita therapy as a narrow medical practice. It is not economical as medical treatment for patients or for physicians either.

But there is a way for Morita's ideas to outgrow their historical

DAVID K. REYNOLDS

limitations. There is a way for Morita therapy to achieve adulthood, I believe. There are risks involved, but the potential rewards are great. Let me paint a word picture for you of this mental health movement twenty-five years from now.

I predict that the word "therapy" will no longer be used for Morita's ideas. We will be talking about the Morita Lifeway or the Morita Lifestyle or Constructive Living or Living Fully or something of that sort. Morita's ideas are practical and useful to everyone, not just to shinkeishitsu neurotics. So they will be applied more broadly outside the medical setting. Morita called his method re-education. The life education aspects of his method will be emphasized twenty-five years from now. Rather than "doctor" and "patient" we will be using words like "teacher" or "guide," and "student."

Physicians will still be consulted to help with diagnosis and treatment of the few people with chemical disorders of the brain like schizophrenia and manic depression, but physicians won't do much of the teaching of this lifeway. They will be too busy with genuine medical problems. Absolute isolated bedrest won't be practiced in hospitals but in retreats like Ashigara Ryo, the Seikatsu no Hakkenkai mountain retreat facility in Japan.

Around the world organizations like Seikatsu no Hakkenkai will offer a wider variety of activities for members. Already there are constructive living groups in Japan for poetry, baking, English conversation, hiking, flower arrangement, reading, sports, social activities, and so forth. The purpose of these groups is not only to develop particular skills but also to bring together people with similar interests and similar problems in their lives so they can learn from one another. Our constructive lifeway must be learned by everyday action as well as by listening and reading. I expect new Seikatsu no Hakkenkai activities like travel groups to different parts of Japan and to other parts of the world, shopping expeditions, home repair classes, dance clubs, writing workshops, bazaars. I wouldn't be surprised if twenty-five years from now there was a Hakkenkai publishing company, Hakkenkai supermarkets, Hakkenkai hotels and *ryokan* inns.

This expansion of Seikatsu no Hakkenkai won't be merely a commercial venture. It will be a demonstration that the Morita lifeway is applicable to all of life—not only interpersonal relationships and the task at hand, but to business and to leisure and to all of self-development and constructive exploration. The shinkeishitsu-character people will be the leaders of this movement for two reasons: (1) They benefit most from turning their attention from inner suffering to constructive activity, so they recognize the value of these life principles, and (2) shinkeishitsu people are persistent and self-sacrificing when they find a purposeful way to live. But the membership of Seikatsu no Hakkenkai will expand to include people who have relatively few shinkeishitsu moments (everyone has some shinkeishitsu qualities, as Morita pointed out). Whether shinkeishitsu or not, a person can perceive the positive and meaningful nature of these suggestions for living.

This broadened approach to Morita's ideas is the path we are following in the United States. There will come a time when Morita's ideas will help to build better understanding and better relations between our countries across the Pacific.

DAVID K. REYNOLDS

PART II

FABLES FOR GROWN-UPS

In *Playing Ball on Running Water* I introduced some stories written for my clients and friends. The stories illustrated some of the principles of constructive living. Here are more tales with the same teaching purpose.

Mineshaft

Clint's father had been trapped in an abandoned mineshaft for as long as Clint could remember. The shaft was so fragile that any attempt to dig out Old Man Geiger would surely bring down tons of earth from the side of Carney Mountain. A small hole dropped twenty feet straight down in the passage where Clint's father lived. That hole was his father's link to the outside world.

As eldest son, it was Clint's job to lower the bucket with his father's meals and water for bathing and other necessities of life. The need to lower candles came less and less over the years. The old miner didn't like reading; his eyes had grown accustomed to the dim spot of light pointing up at the surface world he would never see again.

Clint was sixteen on that crisp autumn day, sixteen and restless and very resentful. What kind of father was that? Hidden away in his dark hole just taking, taking, taking. Other dads played ball with their sons, took them hunting, taught them about cars. Pop only wandered around below ground and crouched by the hole that connected him to Clint's world. Just a nuisance, that's what Pop was. Mom still had to cook for him. Clint had to interrupt whatever he was doing every morning, noon, and night to lower him the bucket. And what did Pop ever do for them? They would all be better off if Pop were dead . . . even Pop himself. What kind of life was that?

Clint put his face into the hole and shouted down, "Hey, Pop! You there?" The old man felt rather than saw the light blocked, and then he heard the words. As the sound reverberated back and forth down the shaft the words distorted, became low-pitched but tinny. He was reminded of the way when he was a kid they used to talk through the cardboard tube from toilet paper or, even better, from a roll of paper towels. When the sounds had completely stopped echoing he lifted his head and shouted upward, "I'm here."

"What you doin'?"

"Nothin'."

"Pop?"

"Yeah?"

Clint started to say something, wanted so much to say something, but his throat tightened up on him. A couple of drops of salt water curled around the rope that dropped into the shaft. Clint and his father sat for a long time in silence.

Once more, "Pop?"

"Yeah?"

"Pop, I'm gonna put a big rock over this hole. I just can't take it no more."

"All right, son. You do what you think best."

A pause.

"Ain't you gonna argue with me, Pop? Ain't you gonna try to talk me out of it?"

"No, son. You do what you gotta do."

Another pause.

"You wanna die?"

"Nope."

"Why not? It ain't no life for a man. Dyin's better than livin' down there."

"Maybe so. Don't know why myself, but I wanna live. Still and all, you do what you gotta do, Clint."

Clint couldn't remember ever talking with his father for so long. The automatic exchange "You okay?" "Fine" had been about the extent of their conversations in the past. He began to see a man down in the mine.

"I can kill you, Pop. Know that?" The words were cold, but they came between gushing sobs.

"Yep."

But he didn't.

As times change and fathers grow old, their sons may take on great power and control in their father's lives. Sons become aware of the limitations and weakness of the men who seemed so strong and knowledgeable before. Clint recognized his power and chose not to exert it hurtfully. Father and son recognized their mutual human qualities in time to avert tragedy.

The Doll Carriage

Renée is in her late twenties now, a pretty girl with good posture and appropriately crossed ankles and studied grace. She is bent on finding a doll carriage. Some would call her quest an obsession. Every weekend she can be found rummaging around in the huge attic of the Victorian house in which she lives searching for an old doll carriage.

Her story begins nearly twenty years ago. Her mother asked Renée to put away the lovely new doll carriage (it was a Christmas gift from both her parents) and help set the table. After the table was set there were other chores to do. Her father left them that evening after dinner; her mother lost interest in living. So it fell to Renée to take care of her mother, her brothers and sisters.

There wasn't much time to play with her dolls in the following days. Being a practical girl she packed away her doll carriage, collapsing it and returning it to its original container, storing it in the attic. And she waited for a better time. During the passing years there was so much to do. Her mother stumbled her way out of depression's fog. Her brothers finished their education. One sister got married. They all appreciated Renée's sacrifices for them. She had been so careful not to cause anyone trouble. There had been slips here and there, but, overall, Renée had been a model child.

Renée was about twenty-six when she felt the urge to find the old doll carriage packed away for all these years. Her brother noticed that she was in the attic shoving around the trunks and boxes. He wondered what she was about, noticed her empty hands as she descended the attic stairs several hours later.

"What were you doing up there?" he asked in that challenging tone so characteristic of his voice and his life.

"Nothing," Renée replied absently. "Just looking for something."

But the next weekend Renée was back in the attic again, and the next, and the next. Always she looked for the doll carriage.

After several months her mother offered to help her search for whatever it was she was looking for. But Renée wanted to do it without assistance from anyone else.

The strange thing was that Renée had absolutely no idea what she wanted to do with the doll carriage if she ever found it. Surely, she had no serious prospects of marriage, didn't feel prepared to have a child of her own. Anyway, the carriage was too small for a full-sized infant. It was completely useless to her, yet she felt impelled to find it.

Some days she searched methodically; some days she flung boxes frantically all over the attic. What could have happened to her childhood plaything? Surely it was here, somewhere in the attic. Perhaps it was hidden under the gowns she had sewn during her teen years. Perhaps it lay beneath the old textbooks from the days when she had finally escaped to a small college up North.

At last, late in her twenty-eighth year, Renée gave up. She sat on the attic floor and cried until there were no more tears to stir the dust next to her hand. She grieved for all that she'd never had and could never go back to find.

Then she went out and found a job that helped kids be kids while they had the chance.

This story was written for someone who seemed to have missed her childhood and was searching for it again. More and more I encounter among my students histories of children who were

DAVID K. REYNOLDS

forced by circumstances to be supportive and adultlike during childhood. Too many had to be like parents to their biological parents. Of course, children should be allowed to be children. But what can be done by those who weren't allowed their childhood when they were young? Renée found a solution.

A Tale of Connection

Once upon a time a couple of molecular compounds were planning to commit marriage. Miss Polyamide Resin (we'll call her Polly) was betrothed to Mr. Epoxy Resin (we'll call him Paul). They were very happy about the wedding, but like all couples they had last-minute jitters.

Polly wondered, "Will he recognize my individuality, my needs?"

Paul wondered, "Will she care about my time, my dreams?"

Both wondered, "Will I still be myself?"

Being molecular compounds of principle they accepted their reservations and focused on their love and trust and united themselves into a larger marital compound. There were still times after the marriage when they thought about their individual identities, but more often they remarked to each other with amazed wonder at how terrific it is to be part of something bigger and more important than the individual parts.

It turned out to be worth giving up some of the self for this greater purpose. In fact, it was downright exhilarating and self-expanding to do so.

As you have guessed, Paul and Polly Resin became epoxy glue when they united their molecules. That means that not only did they stick to each other, they were used to hold other parts of the world together. What a very special task. . . .

This is a story I wrote for a Japanese-American student at the time of her wedding. It is, of course, about independence and merging. It isn't true that Japanese are skillful only at merging themselves in groups and that Americans are skillful only at individualistic independence. We all find ways to do both, purposefully.

Responsibility and Oppression

Once upon a time there was a villager who forced his twelve-year-old daughter to have sex with him. She was treated in the village hospital and released. Her father was brought before the village magistrate. The villager was convicted and referred to a therapist who was required by his profession's ethics committee to treat all clients as though they were twelve-year-old children.

The magistrate required his own son to attend college. The magistrate's son was taught by a professor who insisted that his children attend Sunday School each week. Their Sunday School teacher constrained her daughter to remain a virgin until properly married.

The therapist's son was given a suspended sentence after a vehicular manslaughter conviction because he was only twelve years old. The daughter of the man who was killed by the auto was placed in the care of the Sunday School teacher. The Sunday School teacher never forgave the girl for losing her virginity to the therapist's son when she was eleven. Her dead father had recently been acquitted of a murder charge because he claimed he had been insane at the time, and so he had effectively been twelve years old.

The village in which they lived was on the border between two kingdoms. The village was noted for its strong PTA. The PTA was run for the convenience of the parents and the teachers. The town was run for the convenience of those who governed it. The village hospital was run for the convenience of the hospital staff. The old people of the village all lived together in a special home where they were treated like twelve-year-old kids at summer camp.

There were few traffic accidents but many accidental victims. There were few twelve-year-olds but many who were treated as such. There were few prisons but many prisoners.

This story is about constraints and perspectives. When some members of a society treat adults as though they were children and children as though they were adults, something terrible happens to the victims of that treatment, and to the authorities, too.

Gardening

The old man, bent over by his weeding task, moves slowly from raised row to row. The lettuce and *daikon* radish and Chinese cabbage are surrounded by the irrepressible optimism of koa and nut grass and milkweed. Behind him the beds of yams and peanuts and peas are clear of weeds, the results of yesterday's work. But sprouts of sensitive plant and koa and castor bean are already showing among the string beans and Maui onions he had cleared earlier in the week. By the time he works through today's vegetable beds and tomorrow's formations of zinnias, marigolds, and chrysanthemums, the beans and onions will be fighting for existence with their tough, fast-growing weedy competitors.

Always behind, fighting a rearguard action against the invasion, the old man refuses to hurry. Carefully, carefully he pulls each grassy stalk by hand.

"You've gotta get the roots, you know. They break off at the stem and they're up again the next day."

He cannot win this war. The weeds are inexhaustible. Wave after wave they come, borne on the Hawaiian breeze. Still he stoops and plucks them from the earth, protecting his pampered leafy confederates. If you ask him why he doesn't give up his hopeless course and yield to the inevitability of his garden's return to its wild state, he pauses, puzzled for a moment by the question.

"I don't have to work on the whole garden at once," he observes. "Just this part, now. Then that part, then the next part, over there. Got these weeds to pull now . . . better get on with it."

He returns to his task. Tonight for dinner he will have onions and beans and yams and fresh peas for his persistence. While he eats, the weeds outside will keep on growing.

I am impressed by the persistence of weeds, but more impressive is persistence of people who continue to battle the weeds in their lives knowing that there is no end to the task. This story is about the reassuring prospect that there is only one weed that needs to be pulled at any time.

Hiding Under the Sofa

Whenever times got a little rough Kazuko fled to her haven beneath the sofa. Kazuko was a gray and black cat with a curly coat and a warmth that peeked through her shyness from time to time. All cats show an aloof independence. Kazuko's aloofness seemed painful somehow, as though she would rather have been born a puppy and so better able to express her affection for others.

Grooming is a natural instinct with cats, and Kazuko carefully maintained her furry coat in fine condition. She was less careful about her possessions, however. Her catnip bag, her ball of twine, her rubber mouse, and the scores of gifts bought for her by the Aimes family were usually strewn about the house, cluttering every room. Kazuko seemed to feel more comfortable when the house was in disarray. Perhaps she liked having the familiarity of her things noticeably displayed on every floor of the house. Perhaps she liked to be noticed and scolded by the Aimes children as they scurried about picking up her toys.

Whenever she was scolded she fled immediately to the darkness under the sofa. Crouched there, her tail twitching lazily, she looked out of the darkness with calm eyes at all the bustle and agitation of the real world. How safe she felt under the couch! How confident and in control of her life! Whatever hassles occurred in the light of windows and chandeliers, whatever punishment or aggravation, they couldn't reach the darkness of her safety zone.

Kazuko was not a lazy cat. Her duties as house mouser were promptly and conscientiously carried out. A neighbor cat had once told her that she should never take a day off from her mouse-catching duties. Sick or not, cold or hot, rain or shine, Kazuko made her rounds and kept the Aimeses' house free of rodent guests. In the back of her cat mind were all sorts of questions and worries about her mousing chores. Was she doing an adequate job? If she missed one day would the house be overrun by the pests? What did the Aimes family think of her work? Did her work take too much energy? Should she retire to a more leisurely existence? Would she be bored if she gave up her mousing career?

Every cat needs a haven now and then. Kazuko's problem was that she appreciated the safety of her haven so much that she sought it out more and more. She began to come out only at night to eat and run a fast patrol to check for mice. Her life became narrower and narrower. The Aimes family was concerned. Frankly, Kazuko was concerned, too. And bored. She wanted a world with broader horizons; it's no fun crouching under a sofa all day long while the world outside is filled with tantalizing smells and curious sounds and trees to climb and birds to chase.

Kazuko became so uncomfortable at last that she ventured forth from her hideaway and inquired of her cat friends in the neighborhood what she could do to turn around this self-protective and self-defeating trend. A few of the pampered house cats had gone through similar periods in their lives. One of them recommended that Kazuko begin by retreating to the top of the sofa instead of beneath it.

"At least you can see what's going on in the house that way," a Persian named Forest told her. "I used to get so tired of seeing only the shoes walking back and forth in front of the living-room couch."

For a while Kazuko didn't try out Forest's advice. Unfortunately, she wasn't hurting enough. In time she became so miserable that she was ready to give anything a try rather than continue in the same tedious state. So she leaped on the back of the sofa and watched what was going on about her.

The Aimes family thought that cats belong in areas less delicate than on the back of a two-thousand-dollar sofa. Mr. Aimes scolded Kazuko, and she fled back to her haven. But soon she was out on top of the sofa again. And again she was shooed off. And again she retreated temporarily. The scolding was painful, but her ego was involved now. And there was a game quality to this dispute about the sofa. The whole business was infinitely more interesting than undercouch crouching.

Kazuko gets around much more nowadays. She still flees to her hideaway when a big dog comes into the yard and when thunder roars. Otherwise, she finds that the slightly dangerous world tempts her out of the safe darkness, because security just isn't worth the boredom.

Seeking security alone leads to a narrower and narrower existence. An interesting life, a challenging life, inevitably involves effort and risk.

A Personal Touch

The world of the future was governed by a giant computer—or so it seemed. Its bulk covered several city blocks. Each day hundreds of technicians and programmers and expediters and managers converged on Central C to perform the tasks that kept the input flowing and the output translated into action. The facility was heavily protected. A maze of corridors and offices surrounded the central processing unit. The closer to the center, the higher the security clearance necessary, the deeper and more frequent the psychological scanning, the greater the power—or so it appeared. Around the periphery of Central C were booths with specialized equipment for interviewing people who had important information, for trying World Court cases and arbitrating intercultural disputes.

The system had been worked out centuries before. The safeguards held secure. Mankind prospered. No one paid particular attention to electronics technician Herbert Gray. He arrived at Central C each weekday morning, passed the security checks to his working area about one third of the way into the complex, closed and sealed the door while he performed high-voltage maintenance on the conducting cables and instruments linking Central and several of the interview booths, and returned home each evening to his wife and his *bonsai* trees.

No one had the slightest suspicion of Herbert Gray's vital role in governing the world. Some twenty years earlier Herbert had been selected by his predecessor and Central for this unique job. He had been transferred to Central C from Yokohama C, where he had been in charge of a public information unit. On-the-job training qualified him for a change in specialty. Eventually he was transferred to his current ElecTech position.

What Herbert did, in fact, during each workday was sit within his sealed workstation before a console and help the computer make decisions on matters that required "human input." A computer is quite competent to allocate shipments of grain and route energy resources based on some minimax programming. But it cannot see the world as a human sees it. No strategy of weighing variables can balance compassion and justice in the circuits of a machine. No amount of programmed input can give a computer the "feel" of human existence, the experience of a citizen's life at a particular time and place. So Herbert Gray provided life-informed opinions by answering questions put to him by the computer each day. Sworn to secrecy, he returned home each night and never discussed the monumental influence he had on decision making in his world.

What Herbert didn't know was that at least twenty-three other humans in scattered places around the globe were secretly providing Central C with their responses to similar questions. The computer was, after all, trying to factor out individual biases in order to come up with a truly "human" input. Each felt the responsibility of making a special contribution to humankind. Each thought that he or she alone had been selected for this distinctive task. Each made a mistake now and then. And the work of the world was done.

This story is about limits—the limits of machines and of people.

DAVID K. REYNOLDS

New Opiates of the Masses

The council of devils met to review proposals for keeping the masses sedated and docile. Several new drugs were introduced and accepted. Crucifer reported that institutional religion was losing its effectiveness as a means of turning mankind's attention away from the correctable ills of this life and toward an afterlife. What with the activist religious leaders and the decreased significance of formal religion in people's lives, the effectiveness of religion's tranquilizing ability was increasingly questionable. When asked about the impact of the red-herring project of life-after-life studies and books, Crucifer reported that the passing fad seemed to have produced little misdirection of attention away from everyday life toward religion. The afterlife campaign had been a dismal failure.

Several new approaches were brought up at the council meeting, however. They played upon themes long present in human existence but never previously utilized to their fullest potential. Lustifer suggested that romantic love could be effective in restraining humans from taking effective action to improve their world. She outlined a program of romance novels, serials on television, films, and magazine articles about romances and heartaches of famous people. The attention of many people could be drawn into the web of courtships and breakups, jealousy and possessiveness, anything to avoid serious confrontation with everyday problems. Masshystopheles was enthusiastic about the romantic-love angle because it fitted in beautifully with his own plan to use television as an opiate. He saw that he had to work quickly to avoid the interactive use of televisions with home computers of various sorts. Perhaps more videotaped cartoons, sports, and pornography (in addition, of course, to the romantic soap operas) would tie the viewers passively to the tube.

Some council members thought that the most original idea came from Satiatan. He recommended the use of shopping as a distraction from facing up to the world. What with bargain hunting, window shopping, conspicuous consumption, impulse buying, credit card purchases, and the like, people could be caught up in an artificial world of advertising and consuming. The only flaw the council could find in Satiatan's plan was that people would have to be allowed to actually purchase something now and then in order to stay in the game. But then, it's difficult even for devils to get something for nothing these days.

Several of the proposals passed the council and are being implemented. Others have been set aside for further review and study. The opiates of the masses are varied and sometimes well disguised. They effectively serve to distract humans from doing what needs to be done.

Many people have become skillful at distracting themselves from recognizing their feelings and purposes and from doing what needs doing. Isolated bedrest is one method of forcing them to face squarely these natural elements of reality, without distraction from outside. In everyday life, too, we cannot afford to indulge in these opiates.

DAVID K. REYNOLDS

One Step Forward, Two Steps Back

Sir Jules was a knight with a grand goal in life. He intended some-day to climb the highest mountain in the kingdom of Uckland. His family was proud of Sir Jules's ambition. They looked forward to the day his purpose would be accomplished.

Despite his youth Sir Jules was not an impetuous or foolhardy knight. Very prudently he decided that there was no sense rushing headlong into a mountain-climbing expedition without proper training and preparation. Perhaps, he thought, it would be wiser to start with smaller mountains and work up to the challenge of Mount Summit. So he tried climbing the much smaller Mount Norep.

Part of the way up during the ascent of Mount Norep, Sir Jules became winded. His calves and shoulders ached from the strain of climbing. Being a prudent fellow, he decided that it would be dangerous to overexert himself so early in his climbing career. He turned around and went home for more training.

Months later he began the ascent of Mount Norep once again. This time he carried a lighter pack and wore special supportive shoes. But surprisingly, he found himself winded even earlier than before. His heart began pounding with the exertion. *No use risking some sort of heart attack,* he reflected reasonably as he sat on a boulder by the side of the trail. *I'll try this practice climb another time when I am in better condition.*

There were several moderate-sized hills not too far from the castle. For several weeks Sir Jules carried his pack to these hills and hiked through them. After a while, he had his servant carry the pack as far as the hills. Then he hefted the pack and began climbing. After all, he reasoned, he needn't exert himself on the flat road leading to the hills; he was in training for climbing only. But walking about in the hills became boring. What interested the young knight was a steeper climb. Still, he didn't feel quite ready to tackle Mount Norep yet.

The castle walls were, of course, vertical masses of assembled rock. *You can't find anything steeper than vertical,* thought Sir Jules. He abandoned his hikes in the hills in order to practice scaling the castle walls with rope and spiked boots. Unfortunately, he soon discovered that he was afraid of heights, at least the sheer heights of castle walls. So, being a cautious person, he abandoned that method of training.

If I plan my ascent more carefully in order to avoid the steeper and more demanding paths up Mount Summit, he considered reasonably, *the expedition will surely go more smoothly.* No one would argue with such a sensible course of action. So the young knight worked in his room around the clock poring over maps of the various approaches to the summit.

But as the weeks passed he seemed to grow pale and weak. Day and night he spent in his castle room planning and imagining and wishing for the success of his project. Strangely, each day the mountain seemed higher in his imagination.

In time, people began to wonder if he was really serious about his plan. After all, what he did was merely to sit in his room and talk about what he hoped to do someday. The plans became more and more vague. The date of the expedition became some distant future time when he felt more ready to conquer the mountain.

The mountain won its battle with Sir Jules because the mountain just sat there and so did Sir Jules. Mountains don't have to put one tired, trembling foot before the other in order to achieve success; humans do.

DAVID K. REYNOLDS

On the surface, Sir Jules's thinking appeared circumspect and rational. Yet this sort of thinking kept him retreating from necessary action. It is common in bright people with neurotic tendencies. Such thinking *is* neurotic.

Reflections

Once upon a time in a land far across the mountains a fearsome dragon was terrorizing the kingdom. Many brave young men went out to slay the dragon, called Kyofu by the local villagers, but those who returned at all were crippled and trembling.

Of course, like any other dragon Kyofu could kill with razor-sharp teeth or blows from its powerful, taloned forefeet or the blast from its fiery breath, but it preferred to kill by frightening its opponent to death. Its hideous stare and menacing roar paralyzed many young men into helplessness and breathlessness, with resulting heart failure. Then Kyofu bellowed an exultant roar, having effortlessly disposed of another foe.

But the dragon also enjoyed a good fight. The harder the young men attacked, the more fiercely the dragon counterattacked. Despite all the technological advances in weaponry—the sharpest swords and spears, the finest armor, the strongest bows, the swiftest arrows, and even ergonomic slings—Kyofu's thick hide and formidable strength made any sort of direct human attack virtually suicidal.

Still, the young men showed up to do battle. For they couldn't bear to see the kingdom dominated and exploited by this beast. Kyofu demanded gold and maidens and ceremonies of worship from the villagers. Month by month its appetite seemed to expand. The villagers fearfully brought everything the dragon wanted, knowing the sudden devastation that resulted when Kyofu's whims weren't kept satisfied.

Now it happened that there was a young man named Gen who studied ancient books in the library storage rooms deep in the castle's cellar. From his early teens he had been fascinated with the ideas and hand-drawn illustrations and the old cursive script in the ancient volumes. He had taught himself to read the old works, for the language had evolved to some degree over the years since the books were written.

Gen's friends seldom saw him in the evenings and weekends when they gathered themselves for good times. As they played in the courtyards and courted at the plays, Gen was likely to be found seated between two large candles poring over a huge book propped before him in a sturdy bookstand. His eyes remained strong even in the dim light. The only problems he faced were the sudden sounds of startled rats and the dust that caused him to sneeze violently every so often.

One by one Gen's friends went off to face the dragon. Some went hopefully, some timidly. None returned successfully. Few returned at all.

One day Gen announced to his family that he was ready to take on Kyofu in battle. The announcement came at the dinner table. It took everyone by surprise.

"You're not prepared to do battle," his mother protested. "You are too gentle, too easygoing. My son, you aren't properly trained in the arts of warfare. Lads much stronger and swifter than you have been easily vanquished by that horrid Kyofu. Wait awhile, at least."

She thought she would lose her only son. Tearfully pleading, she begged him to reconsider. But her protests drew from Gen only reassurances that he would be all right.

"I have a secret weapon, Mother, that no one else has ever used against Kyofu. I discovered the power of it in the ancient books. Now that I know the existence of this weapon I *must* use it to challenge the dragon. Can't you see? It's my duty to act on what I know."

And off he went to fight Kyofu with only a small bag over his shoulder and a short sword in his belt. It took no time at all to track down the monster. As Gen walked along the highways, all those passing by pointed over their shoulders in reply to his question about Kyofu's whereabouts. Most of them were fleeing in panic from a recent devastating foray.

Soon he was face to face with his foe.

"Such a tiny, weak thing they send to fight me today!" boomed the dragon. "I could eat twenty of these and still be hungry. Come this way, little boy. I'll frighten you to death and pick my teeth with your corpse."

His knees trembling, Gen approached Kyofu. The scaled monster gave a low roar. The lad fell backward, his face pale. His sword slipped from his hand. The dragon advanced slowly, neck swinging from side to side. It readied its face for a deadly stare.

Gen scrambled back, fumbling in his small drawstring bag. At last he pulled from it his secret weapon and aimed it at the monster. Kyofu advanced three more steps, then wavered and stopped. Bellowing, the dragon lurched forward another step. Then it sank to its knees, rolled on its side, and died.

Gen walked home with the hand mirror resting in his drawstring bag. He carefully replaced the mirror on his mother's dressing table. When the people came looking for their young hero he was already back in the castle's bookcellar, reading and sneezing.

Kyofu means "phobia" or "extreme fear" in Japanese. Such a dragon cannot be fought head on with spears and swords. Trembling and fearful we must face our fears and reflect back to them their true visage. They can be defeated.

The Unicorn and the Menicorn

Where the unicorn has a horn projecting out into the world, the menicorn has a sort of deep pimple, called an introhorn. The unicorn uses its horn to touch things, rather as we use our fingers. The horn is quite sensitive, so the unicorn can learn a lot about a tree or a person just by brushing against it with its horn. The horn is so sensitive that sometimes the unicorn gets hurt—when it nudges something with thorns, for example, or when it bumps against something hard. Still, the unicorn uses its horn quite a lot in its daily life. It is a useful sensory organ.

The menicorn, on the other hand, has its very sensitive dimpled introhorn. But because the introhorn projects inward instead of outward, the menicorn doesn't use it to explore its surroundings. Instead, it grazes passively hoping the wind would blow something into its concave sense organ. The menicorn often wishes that something interesting would fall into its introhorn. Most of the time, however, what falls into the menicorn's introhorn comes from the menicorn itself. Naturally, when it sweats or cries the salt water collects in the introhorn. Strands from its mane and flakes of skin drift into the introhorn, as well. Over the years, the menicorn becomes exceedingly familiar with these aspects of itself. It longs for new stimulation from outside, but it doesn't know how to go searching for new experiences. So the menicorn lives with the overly familiar every day and grows more discontent year by year.

What the typical menicorn doesn't know is that it can reverse the growth of its introhorn and get it to project outward like the horn of a unicorn. It never occurs to most menicorns that they will ever be anything but passive recipients of what the wind and gravity bring their way.

A few menicorns have made the transition. It takes getting out of the pasture and into the woods with all those poking, jabbing twigs and branches. The introhorn gets irritated by all the contact with the bristly underbrush, and it begins to swell. The painful swelling grows outward and, in time, becomes toughened. A menicorn can learn to control the growth of its horn by choosing where to poke it.

You will find that the unicorns with the longest and finest horns were once menicorns . . . though some of them have forgotten.

This story is for self-centered, introverted students. It provides the occasion to talk about what they envy in others, the pain of exploration, and the rewards of getting involved in their surroundings.

DAVID K. REYNOLDS

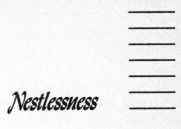

Nestlessness

All the young robins had teetered tentatively out of the nest, stretched their wings with short practice flights, and climbed into the sky to begin their lives of independence. All but Robert. Robert had hatched out last, but only by minutes. Perhaps he was very slightly smaller than his brothers and sisters. Certainly, Robert's voice was no less insistent when feeding time came.

Robert's mother had a special fondness for this fledgling. She thought of him as weak and helpless long after she recognized the capabilities of his siblings. Robert did nothing to change her view of him. Her attitude prompted her to save for Robert the tastiest worms and beetles.

When Robert's brothers and sisters were first scrambling out of the nest, Robert complained of a stomachache. His mother fluffed her feathers and kept him warm in the nest while she kept a sharp eye on the awkward clambering of her other feathered children.

Robert's father was critical of his wife's overprotectiveness. But he knew the value of keeping peace among the treetops, so he said nothing. He twittered a mild grumble to himself now and again.

Robert had grown until he was nearly a year old. He nearly filled the nest. His siblings had flown away long ago. Robert stayed snugly right where he was. Whenever his parents encour-

aged him to try flying he found some reason to avoid the lesson—
a headache, a fear of heights, terror at leaving the security of the
nest, worries about hawks and hunters' guns, and absolute ex-
haustion just considering the possibility of being on his own.

Eventually, the patience of even his long-suffering mother
waned. She came less and less to the nest to feed her son. Robert's
father began building another nest across the park in another elm.
Robert felt hurt and abandoned. Who would love and take care of
him if not his mother? He felt hungry. His wings were under-
developed from lack of exercise. He didn't know how to forage for
himself. He didn't know how to build a nest or find a mate.

"You're not a child any more," his mother had chirped as she
flew away for the last time.

The nest felt dry and cold. It was beginning to fall apart. Lov-
able Robert would have to leave.

"If only I had prepared myself better for this day. I should have
exercised more. I didn't pay any attention to what my folks said
about finding food. Who can I find to take care of me now? I don't
deserve this. It isn't fair. What am I going to do? Nobody loves
me!" Weeping, grumbling, scared to death, Robert edged himself
out of the nest.

There are many Roberts among my students. They have delayed
establishing their independence from family or peers as long as
possible. They haven't picked up many skills beyond the social
skills of being cute, obedient, likable, and nonaggressive. They try
to hold on to childhood social relations by creating symptoms that
keep them helpless. They actually see themselves as helpless. The
world rarely allows them to remain children forever. They feel
unprepared for flying.

Our approach to progressive living reminds these people that
they are no longer children. They must take responsibility for their
behavior as adults. It is sad that we may lose some of our appeal-
ing childlike qualities as we mature, become more competent and
self-sufficient. Nevertheless, the childish adult is a pitiful example
of sculptured ice.

Fellow Humans

Once upon a time in a land far away, some of the women banded together to protect themselves against the males in their country.

"For years men have been oppressing us. They force us to stay at home and care for the children. They refuse to allow us equal representation in the government. They don't pay the few of us who escape into the business world equal wages for the same work men do. They allow us to advance to middle management positions only. They always do as they please and force us to accept their will. How unjust men have been to us throughout the years!" the women exclaimed.

The women held public meetings in the town square, and they met in small groups to support each other in their stand against men.

Carmen Thatcher was walking through the town square on her way home from shopping one day. She saw the gathering of women and stopped to listen to the speeches. She hadn't ever thought of her husband as oppressive. She hadn't considered her role as mother to be a burden forced upon her. She had never considered the issue of equality between the sexes.

Carmen noticed that after hearing the speeches she felt angry at her husband, though she wasn't sure what he, in particular, had done to make her feel this way. Her next-door neighbor, Mildred, began attending meetings of "women's awareness and support groups" regularly. The arguments between Mildred and her husband became louder each week as Mildred learned to be more assertive and demanding of her rights.

About six months later nearly half the women in the kingdom left their villages to begin a feminist commune. They elected their own government, founded their own bank, put on plays about women's rights, and started day-care centers to help care for the children. Mildred was elected Administrator of Health Care.

The men of the kingdom were shocked. Some wanted to send an army out to bring back the women. But wiser heads prevailed. Trade agreements were made with the feminist commune. Tools were loaned.

Strangely enough, the more the men cooperated in the separation, the more women slipped away from the commune back to their home villages. Perhaps the defectors believed that they had made their point and had gained some progress toward equality. Perhaps they thought that separation was too high a price to pay for equality. Perhaps they saw the fallacy of seeing *all* men as evil oppressors and *all* women as fellow conspirators against the male enemy. Perhaps they began to see the flawed character and power hunger in some of their own leaders. Perhaps they just grew tired of only female companionship.

At any rate, within a year the commune was barely surviving, a mere skeleton of what it had been in its first months. And Carmen noticed that the quarreling between Mildred and her husband had lost some of its fire.

This is an oversimplified story about oversimplification. It can be used as a starting point for discussions about equality, feminism, the influence of behavior on feelings, and holding to one's purpose.

DAVID K. REYNOLDS